STEPPING
into the
AQUARIAN
AGE

A Guidebook for the
New Evolutionary Cycle

NANCY PRIVETT

OLD
LION
PUBLISHING

Stepping into the Aquarian Age

Old Lion Publishing
4 Montauk Highway
Westhampton, NY 11977
631-325-3911

First printing 2001

ISBN: 0-9702716-1-1

Library of Congress Catalog Number: 00-92552

10   9   8   7   6   5   4   3   2   1

Manufactured in the United States of America

Cover and interior design by Lightbourne

To Rick who is my warrior of the heart
And to Melia and Rachel who are my blessings

CONTENTS

Introduction ✦ 1

SPIRIT AND SCIENCE: THE ONE FORCE AND THE WEB OF LIFE

The Mystery Schools ✦ 10

A New Relationship: Ancient Wisdom
  and Modern Physics ✦ 14

Modern Physics ✦ 18

Ancient Wisdom Teachings ✦ 24

Bringing Modern Physics/Ancient Wisdom Home ✦ 32

THE PHYSICS OF ANCIENT WISDOM: UNIVERSAL LAW

The Universe's Spiritual Code ✦ 38

The Law of One ✦ 40

The Law of Correspondence ✦ 43

The Law of Vibration ✦ 48

The Law of Polarity ✦ 53

The Law of Rhythm ✦ 57

The Law of Cause and Effect ✦ 61

The Law of Gender ✦ 67

ENERGY LITERACY

The Age of Energy ✦ 76

The Nature of Energy ✦ 78

Properties of Energy ✦ 84

Our Relationship with Energy ✦ 92

THE SYNERGISTIC COMMUNITY OF THE HUMAN ENERGY FIELD

The Human Energy Field ✦ 104

The First Energy Center ✦ 113

The Second Energy Center ✦ 119

The Third Energy Center ✦ 124

The Fourth Energy Center ✦ 131

The Fifth Energy Center ✦ 136

The Sixth Energy Center ✦ 141

The Seventh Energy Center ✦ 146

SYMBOLIC INTERPRETATION: FINDING SPIRITUAL DIRECTIVES IN EVERYDAY LIFE

A Framework for Symbolic Reading ✦ 151

The Literal Level ✦ 154

The Symbolic/Metaphorical Level ✦ 156

The Irrational/Non-Logical Level ✦ 162

The Meaning/Mystery Level ✦ 168

THE CREATIVE PROCESS

Ordering Up Your Life ✦ 172

Superconsciousness ✦ 176

Waking Consciousness ✦ 178

Subconsciousness ✦ 181

Putting Our Creative Power to Work ✦ 184

Steps for the Creative Process ✦ 187

Conscious Use of Our Creative Power ✦ 194

THE HEART OF THE MATTER

Aquarius' Demand for a Strong Heart ✦ 198

What It Means to Have an Open Heart ✦ 200

Focusing Heart Energies Inwardly ✦ 203

A Time of Change as a Time of Testing ✦ 207

A Story to Experience the Power of the Heart ✦ 211

GATHERING THE GIFTS

Buried Treasure ✦ 220

Fulfilling Our Destiny ✦ 223

The Heroic Journeys of Children ✦ 229

Noticing What Is Good ✦ 231

Stepping into Aquarius ✦ 233

Notes ✦ 235

Selected Bibliography ✦ 238

Index ✦ 242

About the Author ✦ 247

INTRODUCTION

As we move through the first century of the new millennium, we are also entering a two-thousand-year astronomical cycle called an astrological age, the Age of Aquarius. The astrological ages are a scientific fact; the language of astrology interprets their symbolism and helps us understand what the age can mean in terms of our daily lives. What is striking about the astrological ages is that the symbolism of the zodiacal sign associated with the age always shows up in a very concrete way on earth. Each age obviously imparts an energy to the planet over a two-thousand-year period. This energy offers challenges for us to explore and experiment with, as well as spiritual lessons which guide us in making decisions about how we think, speak and behave. Each age spurs the evolution of our consciousness and the progression of the ages represents a model that can guide us in going beyond the parameters of knowing ourselves as only physical bodies and minds. The spiritual lessons usher us into the province of the soul and direct us along the pathway that allows us to accomplish the task for which we incarnated.

The execution of this task, sometimes also called our life task, our soul's yearning, and our life mission, brings us the greatest pleasure and satisfaction with our life. It also enables us to give a specific gift to the planet, to model and act upon a quality that makes our earth a better, more conscious, place to live. In the process of fulfilling our task, we undergo a series of tests called life initiations.

As Aquarius settles in, we will each be offered opportunities for initiation. Initiation is an opening, a breakthrough, a vehicle to carry us forward in terms of our evolution of consciousness. It helps us align ourselves with the reason we incarnated, and guides us to find the gift we have to give the planet. When initiation comes, it many times looks like trials, trouble, chaos or loss of control. It requires us to upwell qualities we may not realize we have. And as it does this, it reveals to us our magnificence, the grandeur and sacredness of life and the power of the heart.

What follows is a guidebook that contains information, concepts, instruction and encouragement to direct us on our journey into the waxing astrological Age of Aquarius. This guidebook provides tools which will help us navigate the new age and become proficient in meeting the challenges the new evolutionary cycle will bring. Our journey into the Aquarian Age includes all possibilities, some that we are not yet able to even conceive. We are the vanguard, the forerunners of a new world, predicted for thousands of years to be the Golden Age of the planet. With this in mind, let us step into Aquarius.

✦   ✦   ✦

It was the forlorn aching sound of the wind in the chimney that made her barely able to breathe. It drilled into her very bones, leaving its disturbing song in her marrow. The constant currents of turbulence in the flue caused the fire in the hearth to perform an exuberant dance that threw sparks onto the slate floor close to her feet. Nevertheless, she stood quite still as she was dressed for her journey in warm furs that would leave nothing exposed to the elements. Rawhide laces were pulled tightly and tied and more waterproof resin was applied to her boots. Throughout the procedure, she felt as if she were made of stone.

She had spent the last three days in solitude preparing for her quest. The long hours of inward contemplation had left her with an acceptance, resolve and strength with which she now struggled to reconnect. She had arisen this morning aggressively optimistic and anxious to be off. But as the moment of departure grew near, she felt her determination begin to drain away, her intention waver. She felt confused, not quite remembering why she had agreed to go. Even as she was handed the provisions for her trip, she wondered if she could change her mind and stay here in the warm and familiar abode.

She turned her head at the sound of a heavy wooden door opening. A tiny leather-faced woman shuffled into the room. The woman's long white hair was fine and straight and was tied in several plaits that hung over her shoulders and down her back. She walked slowly toward the younger woman and stood in front of her.

"Maha," the younger woman said, using the traditional greeting of respect.

The elder took the younger woman's chin in her hand. Searching her face for only a second she said quietly, "You are thinking of abandoning the quest."

The younger bowed her head, feeling cowardly.

"It is nothing to be ashamed of," the old woman continued, raising the other woman's chin so that their eyes met. "Even the bravest and strongest, who have been on journeys before, and have come home victorious, many times have a moment of hesitation before starting out."

"I cannot remember why it seemed so important to go," the younger woman admitted in a whisper. She desperately wanted the old woman to give her a reason that would unknot her stomach.

"I cannot help you with that. Only you can feel the yearning that urges you to explore and unravel this mystery. If you cannot feel the pull, then you may be lost before you begin." The old woman's penetrating gaze would not allow the young woman to look down, and the younger one desperately searched the small dark eyes across from hers to find an anchor that would hold her steady.

"Of course, you could always say no," the elder said.

The statement surprised the younger woman, and for a moment she felt a shiver of hope that perhaps she would not have to leave after all. The old woman's eyes continued to hold her gaze, and the room began to shimmer and then dissolve. The younger woman suddenly found herself in the landscape that awaited her outside. An unwelcoming frozen sheet of glacial ice extended in all directions with nothing marring its surface. The sky was a gray steel plate of armor mercilessly clamping down on the arctic terrain. Coldness was so pervasive and insistent that it forced its way through the layers of furs and slowly and insidiously began to creep through her skin.

The bitter land discouraged interference, daring her to try to make a mark upon its frozen surface. She felt the threat of engaging with such a harsh force which could easily seize her and turn her into brittle shards. She could feel herself disintegrating into thin ice feathers, ready to be eaten by the stinging air and assimilated into the unforgiving ground.

She shivered and her body shook to rid herself of the feeling of coldness. The vision began to spin and reform, the frozen landscape melted away, and now she saw those who had decided to say no to the journey. They paraded before her, looking like nothing was wrong, some even smiling, moving through their lives remotely, but not seeming to be in pain. As they flowed across her line of vision, however, their forms became transparent as her eyes pierced through the outer covering of their lives. She began to sense the weight of cold heavy chains which made it difficult to move. She felt her own chest being encircled by a deathly unrelenting grip of tightening vine-like arms. Gruesome, unwieldy encumbrances began to attach themselves to her body and as she looked at those before her she saw that their souls were shriveled and crying out for sustenance. Grimaces bereft of hope were gnarled into their countenances. The stench of despair and disease filled her nostrils and she felt the looming deadly presence of a sickness of the heart that pressed heavily on her own chest and threatened to make her a prisoner of her life. The air became thick and heavy and breathing was such a painful burden, she considered not trying.

Her frightful keening brought her back to the room by the fire. The old woman now held her hands. "You could always say no," she repeated.

The young woman shook her head. "I will go," she said in a monotone. "The ice is more welcoming than a life so dead."

"You have your amulet."

"Here," she said, touching her upper chest, "against my skin."

"Then you are ready, child. It is time."

Somehow she was propelled toward the door. When it opened and the knife-sharp grip of the icy air began to claim her, she was again filled with fear. "What direction do I go?" she implored frantically. "How will I know what I seek?"

But she was already outside. The door was shut behind her.

✦   ✦   ✦

Are we ready?

The Age of Aquarius is moving in.

Trailing ribbons and streamers of science and spirit, technology and ancient wisdom, it is deliberately making inroads, wrapping its robes around our globe and choosing the earth for its home for the next two thousand years.

Some will define its presence as upsetting and disturbing, citing its revolutionary energies of evolution and change. Others will be confused by its demands. Our tongues will trip on the unaccustomed language; we will not understand its new codes.

And at one time or another, even if for just a second, it is probable that we will look back over our shoulders with longing for the familiar, even when the familiar was not all that it could be or even anything like what we wanted.

But Aquarius is no different from any other astrological age. It is just another cycle of our organic, relentless evolution of consciousness. It is another opportunity, another opening, another treasure waiting to be discovered.

If we wish to, we can prepare.

If we are not ready, we can get ready.

We can catch up on old lessons.

We can learn the new vocabulary and be open to new paradigms on which to base our notions of reality.

We can strive to bring out what is best in us.

We can find our broader vision and our inner magic.

We can learn how to create community that supports and enriches us at the same time we support and enrich it.

We can learn, we can change.

If we are willing, we can be aware of the gifts that come with our trials.

If we are willing, we can make the most of a glorious possibility.

✦   ✦   ✦

"What direction do I go?" she implored frantically. "How will I know what I seek?" But she was already outside. The door was shut behind her. The landscape lay ahead and when she turned to look one last time, her warm abode had disappeared. "Where is my home?" she gasped as the wind bit her face. "What lies ahead?"

She spread her hand upon her chest to still her pounding heart and felt the smooth stone of the amulet against her skin. Suddenly the old woman appeared before her once again. "Your home lies ahead," she said, her arm pointing to the unknown vastness. "You will know it when you feel its light."

The young woman was alone. She stood still and desolately stared at what was before her. She pressed the amulet once more and as she did so she felt, as quickly as a glint of sun on water, a whisper of some-thing move inside her chest. Something so profound, so illuminating, so miracle-woven and magnetic, she felt a reverence for her life suddenly pulse through her with a powerful rhythm she had almost forgotten. Her breath caught as she recognized an intangible treasure written into the forbidding landscape. The air turned softer and sweeter; it fed her as she breathed it in. The ice began to glitter and it looked like some-thing holy.

Exhaling, she smiled. She wanted nothing but to put one foot in front of the other and move forward across the snow.

✦   ✦   ✦

Astrological Age	THE SPIRITUAL LESSONS OF THE AGES
Cancer 8000 B.C.E. – 6000 B.C.E.	♋ Live the Law of One ♋ Avoid the shadow of mass consciousness
Gemini 6000 B.C.E. – 4000 B.C.E.	♊ Find the relationship between opposites; understand the Principle of Polarity ♊ Create harmonious relationships
Taurus 4000 B.C.E. – 2000 B.C.E.	♉ Acknowledge matter's basis in Spirit ♉ Be clear about the role of desire and the will in the creative process
Aries 2000 B.C.E. – 0	♈ Become the spiritual Warrior ♈ Balance internal masculine/feminine energy
Pisces 0 – 2000 C.E.	♓ Realize and radiate the power of the heart ♓ Embark upon the Mystic's search for internal Divinity ♓ Release the past
Aquarius 2000 C.E. – 4000 C.E.	♒ Mix Aquarian reason with Piscean heart ♒ Live the Law of One ♒ Evolve from mass consciousness to group consciousness ♒ Negotiate the world of Spirit/matter; become familiar with Universal Law ♒ Become energy literate ♒ Learn to read events symbolically; find the spiritual directive in everyday life ♒ Realize your internal power; become a responsible manager of that power

[handwritten margin note: mystery schools/ religions developed]

The dates for each of the astrological ages have been rounded to 2000 years, from 2160 years. The table does not reflect the waxing and waning periods of each age. These periods are several hundred years each and take place before and after the main two-thousand-year cycle.

Note: The following chapters explore a broader concept of reality than is commonly embodied. You will continually be urged to make leaps from your present model of how the universe works. To take in new, possibly challenging, information may feel okay, or it may feel uncomfortable. If you are willing to stay with the unpleasant feeling of being uncomfortable until it passes, you may be surprised at where it takes you. Some of what is said may seem very familiar; it may resonate within you immediately even though you have never consciously considered the idea before. Some ideas may already be part of your belief systems. Some may sound preposterous. Whatever the case, you are offered the opportunity to risk wading in the waters.

It is necessary to present this information in the language of the Aquarian Age, which is the language of energy. This language has its basis in modern physics, as well as metaphysics. Words and phrases like "energy," "energetic configuration," "vibration" and "frequency" are part of an Aquarian/modern science language, and they will be will be used again and again to relay information and give direction. This format itself helps us to move more gracefully into the new millennium.

As with all learning, the information that follows takes the shape of a circle; everything supports everything else and everything is interconnected. Knowledge given in one section depends on knowledge gained from another, and we may travel a circular path several times, each time stepping outside the boundaries of the first circle in an ever-broadening pattern. This is how knowledge expands into the spiral of consciousness.

One of the concepts which will continue to be addressed is that of the One Force, or what many call God. We have many names to describe this indescribable Essence. Some of them are: Life Force, Creative Force, One Source, Great Source, God, Divinity, Divine Light, Light Force, One Light, Higher Vibration, the Whole, the One, the All, the Mystery, the Secret, the Will-to-Good. Many terms are used throughout, and they are usually capitalized. All are synonymous. They refer to the One Power that creates and sustains the Universe.

SPIRIT AND SCIENCE:
THE ONE FORCE AND
THE WEB OF LIFE

THE MYSTERY SCHOOLS

In every civilization, in every society, we find certain men and women who are attracted to discovering deeper meaning in life. These are questing minds who sense the grandeur, the perfect orchestration and the beauty underlying our life experiences. They are urged to explore life's mysteries, to strive to recognize the hand of Spirit in life and to act on it. These are the members of society who resonate with the possibility that there is much more to life than meets the eye, or any of the five senses.

If we draw a continuum with these seekers of life wisdom at one end, at the other pole sit those who do not feel a sense of Spirit around them. These are people whose desires are disconnected from their hearts, and whose perception of life does not extend beyond that of sensory experience. All of humanity falls somewhere on this continuum, with varying intensities of being driven to investigate the unseen forces and divine principles which organize existence.

It has been the case that the majority of humanity falls nearer to the "non-seeking" pole. This began to shift slightly during the Piscean Age, as the Mystic archetype impelled many to hunger for the experience of feeling the Divine Force alive inside of them. However, the energetic magnetics of the beliefs of the non-seeking group remain stronger because of the greater number. Those at the "seeking" end of the continuum must be prepared to break with these strong magnetics, to develop different attitudes toward life than the non-seekers, and to accept everything that being in a minority group entails. This leaves us with a very committed and powerful group of seekers of life wisdom, whose very existence demands a strength of character.

In primitive societies, such as existed in the Age of Cancer (8000 B.C.E. – 6000 B.C.E.), the sense that life was imbued with Spirit was part of everyday existence. The mysterious reverberations of the Great Mother Goddess were found everywhere in life — from the birth of a baby to the plant that grew and was used for food. Spirit permeated the existence of Age of Cancer humanity, and reverence for this Force was an ongoing daily experience. Tribal ceremonies and rituals were expressions born of this sense of mystery and allowed all members of the tribe to declare and experience more deeply their connection to a Force which permeated and sustained the Universe.

With the advent of the Neolithic Revolution, which saw nomadic culture transform into settled communities based on crop cultivation and the raising of animals, villages began to spring up. The center of these communities was the place of worship, and this was the beginning of the gradual shift from a sense of an "internal religion" to one in which religion was externalized and worship became compartmentalized in the geographic location of a temple or church. Reverence to Divine energies was relegated to centers outside of the self, and the idea of Spirit became more and more removed from everyday experience. This concept of our separation from Divine Force continued through the Age of Taurus (4000 B.C.E. – 2000 B.C.E.), until the Age of Aries (2000 B.C.E. – 0) pronounced that God was the Father and He was outside of, and distinctly separate from, the person.

During the Age of Taurus, those who still felt awe and reverence and sacredness in everyday life longed to pursue experiences which brought insight regarding life's deeper meaning. The thought at that time was that humanity could be divided into two groups: mature minds with a sense of life's sacredness, and undeveloped minds which lacked the yearning to go beyond the superficial. Those of the first group organized themselves into secret groups or cults which were dedicated to the exploration of life's mysteries. These groups are now known as the mystery religions or mystery schools which required would-be members to undergo initiation rituals before being accepted into the group.

The mystery schools pursued universal truth. They were dedicated to discovering magnificence in life and understanding how Divine Law operated on the earthly plane. The teachings of the mystery schools came from a body of ancient wisdom that had been preserved throughout the ages. The origin of the wisdom teachings cannot be pinpointed, but the principles they proffered struck a resonant chord with the seekers of life's mysteries.

The mystery schools taught the doctrine of One God or Force, and how human beings were birthed from the majesty and brilliance of this Force. They ascribed to the idea of eternal life, and trained the members to be responsible, intelligent, patient, courageous and truthful. At first, the teachings were secret because it was believed that the rest of humanity was not mature enough to handle Divine revelations and spiritual wisdom. For mass humanity, the spiritual laws were personified into gods and goddesses.[1] Secrecy was also necessary because the mystery school members were persecuted. The teachings allowed the individual to connect with a mighty inner source of power, which was threatening to those who ruled by means of external power. Especially during the Piscean Age, secrecy became necessary to preserve the teachings in the face of Christians who wished to stamp out what was perceived as "pagan."

Over time, some of the mystery religions became perverted as people used what they learned for sorcery, personal desires devoid of a sense of Spirit, or power over others. However, the persecution of the members of the mystery schools during the Piscean Age served to winnow out those whose dedication to the true intention and principles of the schools wavered. What remained was a cadre of souls who preserved the essence of ancient wisdom so that it could be handed down to future generations.

The established Christian Church was extremely powerful during the

Age of Pisces, especially during the thousand-year period from 500 to 1500 C.E., known as the Middle Ages. Its dogma dictated the nature of people's spiritual beliefs. By the sixteenth century, the Church had become intensely politically involved and was exceedingly wealthy and powerful. This all served to undermine the true spiritual nature of the institution, and as a result, many spoke out against the Church's abuses.

The religious revolution of the sixteenth century known as the Reformation attacked the corruption of the Church and planted the idea that spiritual dicta other than those of the Church might be voiced and accepted. The energies of the Piscean Mystic archetype, mixed with the sparks of the incoming Aquarian dynamics, supported a thirst for spiritual awareness that was available for everyone and did not have to be mediated by a priest or other hierarchical authority. With these forces in effect, for the first time, a statement of mystery school teaching was anonymously published. [2]

From that time forward, the teachings of the mystery schools began to slowly emerge from occult status. Aquarius' modern ruling planet is Uranus, which pushes to have truth come forth, and will illuminate what has previously been unseen or shadowy. With the surge of Aquarian energy that the earth received during the 1960s, the teachings of the mystery schools became more accessible and available. Ancient wisdom still requires dedication and intention to become responsible and compassionate before its secrets are revealed; however, the initiation ceremony is now a personal, internal one which guides the seeker to the Source.

A NEW RELATIONSHIP: ANCIENT WISDOM AND MODERN PHYSICS

The basic teaching of the mystery schools was this: All existence comes from One Source. At the core of everything that we can name in our universe, and everything that exists that we have not yet named, is One Force or Power. This is like saying that there is one basic element from which everything is born — one Divine note, which manifests in myriad ways in both the concrete and non-concrete aspects of life. The rock, the blood vessel, the human personality, the air, the song of a bird, the radio wave, gravity, the emotions of grief and joy, the planet itself: all have at their core the same imprint of an essential all-powerful Source.

This ancient wisdom concept of the underlying unity of existence can be found as the basis of most spiritual philosophies, especially those of the Orient such as Buddhism and Taoism, and western hemisphere native American teachings. Interestingly, during the last century, tenets of ancient wisdom have been uncovered in the scientific arena by physicists, the scientists who attempt to explain the fundamental components of the universe. We find teachings from ancient wisdom mirrored in the revelations of relativity theory and quantum theory of modern science.

Unless we have specifically studied modern science, most of us still have our scientific basis firmly entrenched in a three-hundred-year-old model called "Newtonian physics." Newtonian physics, which was the basis of science during the Piscean Age from the end of the 1600s, explains the universe by breaking it down into component parts, much like a machine. It is a mechanical concept of the world: the universe as a colossal mechanism which is governed by specific laws. Here, everything is composed of building blocks of matter, the basic unit being the atom, a solid particle. The matter which everything exists of is, for all intents and purposes, dead and dense; mind and matter are clearly two separate categories. From this viewpoint, there is a cause for every event and an effect that follows the cause. It is a very comforting paradigm, in that the entire universe can be taken apart, analyzed and described; there is no mystery, no unpredictability. Consequently, there is also no room in this model for a way to describe the vital, mysterious Life Force — the "Something" that causes us to be living creatures, rather than inert lifeless bodies. Newtonian physics relegates the concept of the Life Force to religion, not to science.[3]

In the early 1900s, scientists began to see things that did not fit the Newtonian model. That time period, which reflected the Aquarian Inventor archetype, was prolific with regard to invention and discovery. Einstein's theory of relativity and the arena of atomic physics, or quantum theory, moved to a different drumbeat than did classical physics. The basic characteristics which these new scientific theories ascribed to the universe were characteristics that fractured the Newtonian model: the new science described the universe as having attributes of unity, interconnectedness and change. These characteristics are also descriptives applied to the universe from the viewpoint of ancient wisdom and spiritual philosophies. Here were correspondences between two previously separate areas — science and spirit. Newtonian physics was not broad enough to encompass such a partnership. Yet, what had been believed to be two opposing forces moved into not only compatibility, but what seemed to be twinship, as the statements from physicists began to sound like the words of the mystics.

Listed below are three statements which come from widely varied sources, but all say the same thing. The first is generally attributed to Chief Seattle, an American Suquamish chief, in a speech he made in 1854. The second statement was made by the Nobel laureate atomic physicist Werner Heisenberg. The third is an excerpt from the book *The Essential Kabbalah: The Heart of Jewish Mysticism* by Daniel C. Matt. Read them all aloud, maybe even several times, and let the words really sink in.

> *All things are connected like the blood that unites us all. Man does not weave the web of life, he is merely a strand in it. Whatever he does to the web, he does to himself.* [4]
>   —Chief Seattle

> *The world thus appears as a complicated tissue of events, in which connections of different kinds alternate or overlap or combine and thereby determine the texture of the whole.* [5]
>
>   —Werner Heisenberg

> *The sublime, inner essences secretly constitute a chain linking everything from the highest to the lowest, extending from the upper pool to the edge of the universe. There is nothing — not even the tiniest thing — that is not fastened to the links of this chain . . . . The entire chain is one. Down to the last link, everything is linked with everything else.* [6]
>   —Daniel C. Matt

If we were to draw a picture to represent the idea set forth in these statements, we would probably draw something that looked like a spider's web, connecting every person with every person, every thing with every thing, every event with another. We would end up with a picture of energetic passageways connecting everything in our universe. Of course, this concept is being manifested in our world right now in the form of the computer Internet. The words "web" and "net" are both good descriptions which depict the idea of an interconnected universe which emerges from one Whole.

It is interesting that we find the universe described in this way in three such seemingly diverse areas as Native American philosophy, atomic physics and Jewish mystical spirituality. Yet, if we looked further, we would find the same kind of statements from eastern spiritual philosophies, ancient wisdom texts and accurate translations of the Bible. The correspondences themselves illustrate the interconnection of which we are speaking. From all of these provinces comes the same message: the universe is not made of separate, unrelated parts (as science previously told us); rather the universe is one Whole and everything is related to everything else.

When we think of the universe in these terms, it is easy to see that an event or occurrence in one part of the web would naturally have an effect on the whole web. The greatest impact might be felt nearest the occurrence itself; but eventually, like the ripples from a stone dropped in a pond, the energy of the occurrence would reach even the farthest shores.

Here is what this means for our everyday lives: our thoughts and deeds of kindness, compassion and love have a beneficial, healing effect on those closest to us — our family and friends. However, the ramifications of manifesting these qualities do not stop there. Ultimately our positive thoughts and actions have a healing effect on the whole world.

Conversely, our thoughts and deeds of hatred, separation and cruelty have a negative, wounding effect most powerfully on those closest to us. This is true even if the negative thought we have or deed we do is not directed at those closest to us. A big impact will still be felt by our family and friends, simply because of their relational proximity to us. Because of the web of life, our negativity then carries darkness to the entire planet.

MODERN PHYSICS

Unity, Interconnectedness and Change

Because of the new relationship between science and spirituality, it is possible to use science as a sturdy and comfortable shoulder on which to lean, as we examine a model of the universe that could change our basic beliefs of what life is about. Science has traditionally given us the belief systems on which we build our concept of reality. We do not have to make a leap of faith to "believe in" science; it has become the vehicle which provides us with the necessary foundations for new paradigms of what life is about. Newtonian physics was Piscean Age science; Aquarian Age science is the science of modern physics which began to break through in the beginning of the twentieth century.

The two basic theories of modern physics are the complex relativity theory and quantum theory. In 1905, Albert Einstein published the first of two papers on the theory of relativity, and began an excursion into new paradigms of scientific understanding outside the classical Newtonian model. Relativity theory demonstrated unity between what had been assumed to be distinct; specifically it demonstrated the unity between matter and energy, space and time, and gravity and acceleration.

Relativity theory also changed the perception of what matter was composed of. Rather than building blocks of material substance, relativity theory demonstrated that <u>mass is really energy</u>. This changed the concept of matter as being composed of substance that was essentially lifeless to matter composed of substance that had <u>patterns of movement and frequency.</u>

Quantum theory, which has to do with subatomic particles smaller than molecules and atoms, had its foundation laid in 1900 by Max Planck. Quantum physics found that <u>subatomic particles</u>, rather than being solid and inert, <u>behaved in the framework of probabilities of *connection with each other*</u>. Quantum theory defined matter as <u>moving and changeable energy whose very nature was to connect and relate</u>. From quantum physics came a new view of not only matter, but of the whole universe. In *The Tao of Physics*, a book which explains in detail the specific correlations between modern physics and the ancient teachings which are the basis of mysticism and the core of the Eastern religions, Dr. Fritjof Capra states:

> *Quantum theory forces us to see the universe not as a collection of physical objects, but rather as a complicated web of relations between the various parts of a unified whole.*[7]

Werner Heisenberg, a German physicist and Nobel laureate, stated that the <u>whole world appears as a tissue of interconnecting events, the movement of which determines the nature of the whole</u>. Dr. Heisenberg was the formulator of something called "uncertainty principle," a term whose name alone indicates that it certainly does not harmonize with Newtonian physics' concept of a predictable universe. Uncertainty principle influenced not only quantum theory but also philosophical thought.

Relativity and quantum theories defined the dynamic nature of the universe — a universe in which change and movement are inherent. Dr. Capra states that the unification of space and time in relativity theory implies that matter cannot be separated from its activity. This is the universal Law of Vibration from ancient wisdom which says that nothing is static; everything moves and vibrates. In this reality, change is an inherent characteristic of life. The Law of Vibration is illustrated by Dr. Capra's statement:

> *Atoms consist of particles, and these particles are not made of any material stuff. When we observe them, we never see any substance; what we observe are dynamic patterns continually changing into one another — a continuous dance of energy.* [8]

Relativity and quantum theory were not merely new discoveries in the world of science; they demanded an entirely new perception of how the universe works. Now, in order to describe the universe, physicists were using words and phrases formally relegated to the world of spirituality and mystical concepts of reality. The universe was being described as a web of energy. Not only that, but this energy, by its very nature, changed continually and this was to be expected. The independent parts of the web were unalterably connected to the whole web, and constantly interrelating with each other. In fact, in order to define the parts, they had to be described through their connection to the whole. Notice the many correlations to the energies of the astrological sign of Aquarius and its ruling planet, Uranus: acknowledging the Oneness of all life and the collective situation of humanity (unity); co-existing and sisterhood and brotherhood (interconnectedness); and, changes (dynamism).

The basic concepts of quantum physics are not limited to the very small world of subatomic particles, but extend to the "larger" areas of science, like cosmology, which is the study of the universe as a whole, and astrophysics, a branch of astronomy which is a study of stars, galaxies, black holes, cosmic rays and the like, and the laws that govern them. Here the metaphysical principle of "As above, so below; as below, so above" is again demonstrated; what is true for the very small worlds is also true for the very large ones.

It is inevitable that all areas of science, including medicine, will be influenced and transformed by the three basic tenets which modern physics uses to describe reality: there is a unity behind everything;

everything is interconnected; everything moves and changes. We can see how the new area of psychoneuroimmunology, the mind/body connection in medicine which demonstrates the connections between the brain, endocrine and immune systems, is based on the interconnecting qualities of life. Also, the term "holistic," now being applied more frequently to issues of health care, encompasses the idea of the Whole.

Holography and Implicate Order

Let us look at other areas and theories of modern science which demonstrate metaphysical principles. Holography is an area in which it is easy to see how science is moving into what might be called a mystical realm. A hologram is a three-dimensional photographic image which is produced from the interference pattern of a split laser beam. An extraordinary property of a holographic film is that even if it is cut up into pieces, each of the pieces carries the whole three-dimensional image. In fact the word "hologram" comes from two Greek words: *holos* which means "whole" and *gram* which means "message." In his book, *Vibrational Medicine*, Dr. Richard Gerber likens this property of holograms to a characteristic of human cells, every one of which carries the DNA material which contains all the information needed to make another complete human being, the concept used in cloning. The holographic principle is expressed in ancient wisdom as: Every piece contains the whole.

Modern physicists have extended holographic theory to describe how the universe works. If a piece of holographic film can contain all the information in the entire film, perhaps each piece of the universe contains all the information of the universe. Nobel prize-winning physicist David Bohm used the term "holomovement" to describe this concept. His theory of implicate order describes a universe in which vital information is holographically enfolded in every aspect of existence. In a *New Dimensions* radio interview, Dr. Bohm stated:

> *Implicate order suggests that wherever you are is in contact with the Whole. We emerge from the Whole and the quality of the Whole is in each element.*[9]

Dr. Bohm's description of the universe contains the image of a conscious, ordered, dynamic, interrelating web of life. As we examine the wisdom teachings in the next section, we will see that Dr. Bohm's description perfectly correlates with ancient wisdom.

Morphogenic Field Theory

Another theory developed from the basis of an interconnected universe is Dr. Rupert Sheldrake's morphogenic field theory. Dr. Sheldrake is a British theoretical biologist and he defines morphogenic fields as invisible organizing fields of energy connecting different species. According to the theory, as each member of a biological species learns a new behavior, the species' morphogenic field shifts, little by little. As the behavior is repeated, something called "morphic resonance" builds up, and the entire species is affected by the new behavior in more and more noticeable ways. An example of this would be someone breaking a world's record in sports; once the previous "barrier" is broken through, it becomes easier for others to do the same. We see this theory at work in adverse ways also. In 1998 a rash of firearm attacks on schoolchildren by a classmate became prevalent. After the first incident, a string of other similar incidents occurred throughout the United States.

The ramifications of Dr. Sheldrake's theory are astounding because they mean that in whatever way we empower ourselves to live consciously, we allow the possibility for that same movement in every other member of the human race, and indeed magnetically "pull" other members toward that behavior as we continue living in an empowered way. Conversely, in whatever ways we disempower ourselves by not living consciously in accordance with spiritual law, we affect others in a negative way. This gives us a great responsibility, as well as a tremendous power. We sometimes forget that how we hold our energy, that is, how consciously we live, is the most powerful way in which we can affect others. The strongest effects will be felt in those closest to us; but again, just like the ripples in a pond from one stone thrown, eventually the effects are far-reaching. It is no wonder that the impact of Dr. Sheldrake's theory is being compared to the impact of Darwin's theory of evolution.

What modern physics constantly reveals is that the universe cannot be understood as separate components, but only as a dynamic living Whole of interconnected and interrelated phenomena. This concept defines all aspects of reality — what we call our physical existence — as instinctively *active* and *alive,* naturally *connected* and constantly *relating.* These are adjectives we use to define the Life Force itself; now we are applying them to all of reality — solid, material existence, as well as the intangible, invisible aspects of life.

ANCIENT WISDOM TEACHINGS

Basenote of Ancient Wisdom: Recognizing Spirit Everywhere

Modern physics actually attempts to do exactly what the wisdom teachings do — reveal the true way the universe works, which means understanding matter at very deep levels. Classical physics, in contrast, is more concerned with predicting and controlling matter. It is not inappropriate to regard the tenets of modern physics and ancient wisdom as mirrors of each other.

The essence of the wisdom teachings can be found at the core of many spiritual philosophies, especially those of the Orient, as well as the spiritual beliefs of certain native American cultures. Many Western religions have, either intentionally or unintentionally, throughout their history, covered up, dismissed or adulterated the wisdom teachings. The most probable reason for this is that ancient wisdom can give the individual tremendous personal power and freedom (as well as tremendous responsibility) and, in the Middle Ages especially, religious institutions became involved with trying to acquire that power for themselves.

Our re-education in ancient wisdom must begin with the basenote of all the teachings: an understanding that Spirit is not something that is far away and separate from the earthly plane. The importance of acknowledging and embodying this concept, which is called the Law of One, is crucial to moving forward in the new evolutionary age. As the astrological ages progressed, we were given the lessons of the Law of One again and again, in order to integrate it as deeply as possible.

Because we think in dualities, it is natural to construct two poles — the world of matter and the world of Spirit. It is even helpful to do this in order to grasp certain concepts and understand our own behavior. But when all is said and done, we need to go back to the basenote from the Age of Cancer and begin to embody the Law of One, the spiritual principle which lets us know that Spirit is not a separate "world," but pervasively present everywhere.

In the holistic model of a human being, we define four levels: the physical, the emotional, the mental and the spiritual. Thinking of these four separate levels helps us to understand that we are more than physical bodies and physical existence, and that our spiritual lives are just as important as our physical, emotional and mental ones. But the truth is that the physical level *is* Spirit, the emotional level *is* Spirit, and the mental level *is* Spirit; the spiritual level is not separate but is present in the other three. We *are* Spirit, we live spiritual lives, and there is nothing that we do that can be separated from Spirit.

This means that everything we do has its basis in Spirit. If we pick up a fork to eat, Spirit is behind the action. What we call personal activity is really Spirit expressing itself through us. If we feel an emotion, Spirit is the impetus behind the feeling. Every one of our thoughts is fueled by Spirit. There is nothing we do, think, feel, or say that comes solely from us as individuals; everything has its basis in Spirit because all existence has a basis in Spirit.

Spirit is the Power, the Force behind everything. If it is the essence of the universe, then it *is* the universe and nothing can be separate from it. Our three modes of human expression — reason, will and emotion — all emerge from Spirit. This gives us quite a powerful backup supporting anything we think, do and feel. It is our ability to open to this "fuel source" that determines the amount of Power we can express. So any idea that we conceive, comes from Spirit; the more we can allow this Force to flow through us, the more plentiful and powerful will be our ideas. Any time we use our will, the impetus for it comes from Spirit. When we define our will power in terms of Spirit, it is infinite. When we believe that we exert our will personally, it means that we are not allowing the full power of Spirit to flow through us. And when we feel any emotion, the force of that feeling has its basis in Spirit. The strongest feeling that we as humans can experience, the one with the most transformative power, is the Force of love. Ancient wisdom teaches that whenever we experience the state of being we call love, we are the closest we can get to truly knowing the Spirit from which we are birthed.

Spirit Can Be Misdirected

Of course, there are questions about negative actions, negative thoughts and negative feelings. Are these, too, fueled by Spirit? Surprisingly, the answer is yes. Another name for Spirit (and remember that there are too many to count) is the Will-to-Good, meaning that Spirit is a Light Force that has only our best interests as its focus. It is a Force which wants us to experience the very best things that we can think of — things like joy, abundance, happiness in relationship, and the unwavering presence of unconditional love. The more we open ourselves to Spirit, meaning the more we recognize Spirit inside of us, the more we can let its impetus urge us to these states of being. However, as human beings, we have free will, the power to choose, and because of this, we have the choice to misdirect the Force of Spirit which flows through us.

We can think of the way Spirit comes through us cleanly as a clear pathway through a lovely landscape; when we exercise our freedom of choice not to allow ourselves to be so filled with Spirit, the pathway becomes twisted and distorted, and the landscape turns frightening and desolate. We forget that Spirit is the Will-to-Good, or we do not believe it, and we close off the open paths for this Divine Force to flow through us and emanate from us. We set up roadblocks, we impose detours, we rescind our invitation to Spirit to dwell fully in us, we refuse to recognize our Divine origins. We do these things because we are afraid, because belief systems we hold tell us that we are limited with regard to the amount of Spirit we can allow to radiate from us. Unconsciously, as well as consciously, we buy into belief systems which dictate that we are not good enough to hold that much Light, not worthy, not lovable, not One with a Force which would give us everything we need. We forget that Spirit is our Origin, is our Home, and that our true longing is to let It flow through and emerge from our human form as fully as It can. And so the Force that could fuel our love, we use instead to fuel our anger and our hatred. The Force that could fuel our own expression of will-to-good, we use to fuel our will-to-evil. The Force that could fuel our inherent heroism, we use instead to fuel our degradation.

When we use Spirit to fuel our distortions, our shadow sides, we are in a state of what healer, teacher and author Barbara Brennan calls "profound forgetting." We forget the true nature of the goodness of Spirit and we forget that we naturally inherit this nature, since we are birthed from Spirit. We forget that every element of our existence is imbued with the potential to hold this Force of infinite goodness. We become lost, mired in this earthly dimension, not recognizing that Treasure is all around us, not seeing the Castle of Light even though we are standing in the middle of it.

One way we can transform our "forgetting" into remembering is to follow a disciplined course of study of the ancient wisdom teachings, which are available right now. The wisdom teachings, as well as other courses aligned with the Will-to-Good, can help us to open our eyes to recognize that the Castle of Light is available for us to reside in, every minute of every day.

Emerging from the Whole

Ancient wisdom teaches that everything springs from One Substance, One Source, or as the physicist Dr. Bohm put it, "emerges from the Whole." Characteristics of the One Substance are that it is an Intelligence that is mysterious, infinite, eternal, all-powerful, ever-present and most sacred. Of course this is our concept of God, or Divine Force. The many names for the conscious, essential One Source, that elusive Something that gives us Life and holds the universe in place — names like God, Divine Force, One Force, One Substance, One Source, the All, Spirit — are interchangeable. The reason for the vast number of appellations is that the One Source is so beyond human linear comprehension, that it is actually unnamable. Every time we try to translate it and give it a name, we actually limit our perception of it, and of course the One Source is limitless. So we use many names to try to describe it adequately.

When we substitute the word "God" for the One Source, it is necessary to be aware of any ways in which our personal definition of God inhibits our ability to understand clearly the magnitude of the One Source. The definition of God that we garner from religious teachings must be influenced by dogma. For us, the word God may include energies that are patriarchal, tyrannical, unmoving, or in some way limit our own power or authority. Because of these inherited, tribal beliefs about God, it is sometimes easier to simply let go of the word for now, and use another phrase to describe the Divine Force from which we are birthed. This will allow us the potential to move into an *experience* of the One Source that will not be restricted by preconceived assumptions.

The teaching of One Source at the root of everything describes a universe which comes from one Whole. Our word "Universe" is from words meaning *taken from one*. Let us look again at the statement of the physicist David Bohm, now sounding like a mystic as he describes his theory of implicate order.

> *Implicate order suggests that wherever you are is in contact with the Whole. We emerge from the Whole and the quality of the Whole is in each element.*

Now let us substitute the word "God," and then the word "Spirit," for the phrase "the Whole" in Dr. Bohm's statement. Let us also substitute the phrase "each of us and in all things" for the phrase "each element." Read these new statements aloud.

> *Implicate order suggests that wherever you are is in contact with God. We emerge from God and the quality of*

God is in each of us and in all things.

Implicate order suggests that wherever you are is in contact with Spirit. We emerge from Spirit and the quality of Spirit is in each of us and in all things.

As we speak the words, we are speaking the basic teaching of ancient wisdom. We are also speaking the language of the new Aquarian Age.

Interconnectedness

Because all humans are birthed from the same Source, from Spirit, we are all related. We are interconnected from our very creation. Going a step further, if the One Force is the Source of *everything*, then *everything* is related. There is an essential connection between you and me, and the trees, the animals, the mountains, the planets, all of life, all of existence; this essential connection is one of the most sacred things we can experience.

North American indigenous cultures are aware of this unity and interconnectedness, and their view of the universe — their brand of physics — contains the essence of the ancient teachings. Here again are the words attributed to Chief Seattle, the great Suquamish chief:

All things are connected like the blood that unites us all. Man does not weave the web of life, he is merely a strand in it. Whatever he does to the web, he does to himself.

Likewise, the words of the shaman Black Elk illustrate the belief in the unity and interconnectedness of the universe:

I was seeing in a sacred manner, the shapes of all things in the spirit, and the shape of all things as they must live together, like one being. And I saw that the sacred hoop of my people was one of many hoops that made one circle, wide as daylight and as starlight, and in the

center grew one mighty flowering tree to shelter all the
children of one mother and one father. [10]

Here is the web of life and the interconnectedness quantum physicists talk about to describe the universe. Here are the same concepts
which form the basis of many eastern spiritual philosophies, the same
concepts of native American spirituality, the same concepts from
ancient wisdom, the same concepts being energetically brought to us by
the symbolism of the astrological age of Aquarius.

The implications of such a belief system are enormous and far-
reaching. Based on a philosophy of unity and interconnectedness, we
would understand that if we hurt someone else, we hurt ourselves in the
same way; if we abuse our planet's resources and gifts, we similarly
abuse ourselves. Any time we "rip the web," the eventual consequences
to us, personally, are intensified feelings of vulnerability, powerlessness,
loneliness and more separation from the vibrancy of life. Looking at the
other side of the coin, good deeds sent out to others would make us feel
good; strengthening the web would make everyone feel stronger and
more powerfully compassionate.

We can set forth the ramifications of an interconnected universe that
comes from One Source in the following way.

1. Whatever I do, think or say has an effect on you; whatever you
   do, think or say has an effect on me.

2. Whatever I do, think or say will have the strongest effect on
   those around me, my family and friends; this is true for both negative and positive thoughts, words and deeds.

3. Whatever I do, think or say eventually affects the entire planet
   and, in fact, the entire universe.

4. My positive deeds make the world a better place; my negative
   deeds make it a more difficult place.

5. If life is difficult, I must ask myself the question: How am I con-
   tributing to the difficulties?

To evaluate ourselves according to these principles is the beginning of the creation of a synergistic society, participating in a group consciousness, one in which everyone is respected as having the Divine spark of Spirit at his or her core.

Dynamism

Like modern physics, ancient wisdom also teaches that movement and change are inherent in life. This is called the spiritual Law of Vibration and can be simply stated by saying that the universe is never at rest, but rather constantly in motion. Because the Universe is dynamic patterns, change is the rule rather than the exception. This imparts a natural transformative, evolutionary quality to the Universe, and is a very powerful aspect. What it translates into for our daily lives is that change will come, whether we embrace it or not, and resisting change, an action in opposition to the natural state of the universe, will have its necessary consequences. Illness and crisis are usually our messengers to alert us to the fact that we are being given an opportunity to explore some aspect of our lives which can be transformed in order to enhance the quality of our lives.

As we can see, modern physics is "discovering" nothing new; it is merely bringing to light ancient wisdom which needs to be integrated into the planetary consciousness. Because of science's solidity as an indicator of what is real and what is not, physics is the perfect vehicle to make us aware of ancient wisdom. The wisdom teachings have been presented to us throughout the ages and they can be derived, or read, in any event, an example of Dr. Bohm's theory of implicate order. In this way, any event or circumstance can be evaluated from new perspectives based on true universal law.

BRINGING MODERN PHYSICS/
ANCIENT WISDOM HOME

The Aquarian Age impels us to begin thinking in terms of energy as the basis of our universe. Remember that the Aquarian glyph represents different forms of energy and that the symbolism of Aquarius is associated with the new sciences. In addition, Aquarius represents the urge to find the Divine everywhere, all around us. Using modern physics/ancient wisdom as a basis, we can begin our homework.

The chair in which we sit, the air around us, our bodies, even our thoughts — all are energy waves and configurations, each with a specific structure, frequency and flow. We can imagine the different ways that energy presents itself as different colors, different sounds, different patterns and different movements. To the naked eye, these energy patterns are "invisible"; the technology that will give us a clear picture of such patterns is still being developed. The technology will come as we simultaneously recognize our own ability to see such energy patterns with our human eyes. However, the patterns are still able to be perceived by us in some fashion, if only on a very subtle level. This subtle perception is a different kind than we are used to. Our culture is full of loud, noisy, short-attention-span stimuli and distractions that speak at us, usually in attempts to sell us something. Perceiving energy patterns requires a quiet centering, a drawing in of our energy, in order to let it radiate out naturally to explore what it is we focus our attention on. Centering and focusing our attention require disciplined practice. There is no substitute for this practice, even if we have an inherent ability to read energy.

As we quiet the linear mind, we can begin to sense the quality of the vibrations around us. We become open to the most subtle nuance, the quietest insight. We can pay attention to how our physical body responds to the vibrations in our immediate environment, *experiencing* how the body feels, allowing images to arise from this feeling and then using the linear mind *in service of Spirit*, by translating the experience of the body into language. We begin to name the quality of vibration we are experiencing and associate it with the images and archetypal symbols which are presented to us in the non-linear state.

We can practice perceiving human energy patterns by sensing the energy from someone in physical proximity to us and then translating what we are sensing. We can translate by drawing or painting the energy, singing the energy, moving our body like the energy or trying to put the description into words. We have all had the experience of meeting someone and, for no apparent reason, either feeling uncomfortable with the person, or attracted. The repulsion or attraction depends on how the energetic configurations we hold in and around our body mesh with the configurations of the person whom we meet, how our field of energy waves and that of the person either harmonize or clash, flow in the same direction, or do not. We must remember that an attraction to another does not necessarily mean that the way in which our field meshes with the other person's field is positive and healthy. When the victim's field of energy meets the perpetrator's field of energy, for example, the fields will mesh very easily, and this can feel very *familiar*, and thus comforting, to both people. Conversely, we can actually feel threatened upon first meeting a stranger because his or her field is organized in a way with which we are not familiar. "Unfamiliar" does not necessarily mean "bad." The unfamiliarity may be due to the fact that the person has just dismantled some defensive behavioral pattern and we are still immersed in the very same pattern ourselves.

When we hold a rock in our hand and look at if from the old scientific viewpoint of Newtonian physics, the rock is a mass of solid, unmoving, unchanging material, certainly having no connection with "life" or "life force," both of which imply some kind of movement or urge. The rock is certainly different from a tree, or a human body. How willing are we to risk the insecurity and discomfort of moving into a new way of thinking? Can we look at the rock from the viewpoint of modern physics? If we can, we allow for the possibility that the rock is made of energy which moves, moves in certain patterns, holds certain frequencies and has a resonance, a relationship, with our own energy. The rock is no longer constant and invariable. Dr. Capra uses the descriptive word "mutable," which means "able to be changed," to describe solid matter in terms of modern physics. This is an extremely powerful alchemical concept which we are now applying to dense matter as we try to sense the rock as "mutable substance." If we can focus our awareness, at some point we will begin to pick up the most subtle nuances of Spirit in what used to be considered "not alive."

Putting our hand against a tree, we see if we can find the same sense of Spirit in what we call a "living" object. This should be somewhat easier since we already have a perception of a tree as "alive." With focused concentration, we can begin to uncover the "aliveness" in everything around us, and sense that it is aliveness from the same Source. This is not a linear experiment; in fact, the active, linear mind will be an impediment to sensing Spirit. Yet, what may seem to be a silly, trivial exercise can lead us to a profound experience of understanding the unity, interconnectedness and dynamism of life.

We can picture every aspect of life represented as energetic configurations joining to connect in a web of energy that spans our entire universe: complex, beautifully detailed patterns of diverse waves of energy merging and resonating, joining and harmonizing with each other. Our words, our deeds, our thoughts, our human bodies, merging with all other life forms, with the mountains, the rivers, the vast sky, and on outward to the planets, the stars. Everything from the same Source and everything linked, so whatever happens in one part of the web affects the whole picture. If one part of the web begins to shimmer and glow from an act of kindness, energetic waves of the same vibration are sent throughout the entire web. If one tiny piece of the web is torn or vibrating inharmoniously from one negative thought, this too sends its repercussions throughout the entire web. We are picturing what Chief Seattle knew to be true: we are all One.

Of course, we now have the outpicturing of this concept of the universe as an energetic web in the Internet. Here is the Aquarian Age providing us with a very concrete, visual and experiential example of a model of how life works. Distance is irrelevant on the Internet; we connect with each other almost instantaneously in spite of geographic location. This is exactly how energy works, how prayer works, how thoughts work, how Spirit works. We only believe we are separate and isolated and cannot make a difference; we actually have energetic passageways available to connect with everyone and everything in creation. On a smaller level, we have the same kind of communication network in our physical bodies, as our thoughts are instantaneously communicated to our cells and interpreted literally.

As modern physics begins to trickle into our consciousness more and more, we will begin to shift our views about how our universe works. The principles of modern physics will inevitably become the principles on which we base how we live our daily lives; and they will harmoniously integrate with and mirror the ancient wisdom that is the basis of spiritual living. However, as always, we do not have to wait for the rest of society to incorporate new models for living; we can move into a new paradigm on our own, at any time. Working to increase our consciousness at a faster pace than society is always an option.

Our concept of reality will begin to shift, if it has not already, more and more into the merged belief system of science and Spirit. Science will allow us to move into the Aquarian concept of unity and interconnectedness; science will allow the Uranian energies of dynamism to be included in our definition of what it means to be alive. If we allow ourselves to be taught by the dance of subatomic particles, we will begin to awaken to a universe in which the breath of Spirit is seen in everything, everyone, everywhere, at all times. Science will enable us to define ourselves as One Spirit, inevitably connected with and related to every other human being. It will force us to winnow out any belief system we hold that does not conform to the Law of One, which means any belief that keeps us behaving in separatist, alienated, discriminatory ways.

And that should cause quite a stir on the planet.

THE PHYSICS OF ANCIENT WISDOM: UNIVERSAL LAW

THE UNIVERSE'S SPIRITUAL CODE

We have just seen how the properties which modern physics assigns to an energy-based universe are the same properties that the ancient wisdom teachings use to describe Spirit. Studying either energy or Spirit leads us in the same direction, which is the direction of the new millennium. The Aquarian Age urges us not only to define life from an energy-based perspective, but also to understand Spirit and see it in life all around us. In this section we will study a spiritual code which helps us to understand how Spirit/energy works in our three-dimensional reality. Understanding the code helps us to navigate across the Piscean Age-built bridge between the worlds of matter and Spirit.

When we want to know more about how Spirit works in our physical plane, we can look to a spiritual dictum called universal law. Also called divine law or spiritual law, the universal laws are principles derived from ancient wisdom which describe how the universe operates. Universal law delineates eternal truths about life. The laws never change, and we find them constantly working everywhere, in every facet of our lives. Every single event can be reduced to universal law, and can be read as either in harmony with universal law or in dissonance with it. Universal law can help us understand events and people at levels deeper than the superficial, and it is invaluable when attempting to translate events in order to decode their spiritual directives.

Being in Dissonance with Universal Law

When we move with the energy of the laws of the universe, we have the power and force of Spirit behind us; when we ignore essential truths, we are in an unnatural state. Non-cooperation with the law of the universe results in consequences. These consequences may not be immediate, but they will most assuredly occur. They are usually pain, crisis, trauma or discomfort of some sort, designed not only to get our attention, but also to give us the perfect, personalized opportunity to become more conscious with regard to the way Spirit works and how we can work with It.

Being in dissonance with universal law is like pushing against the weight of the whole universe. When our consciousness has evolved to a certain point, we will be more aware of when we are out of sync with the laws that govern the cosmos. We will experience our dissonance as a physical, emotional, mental and spiritual burden. If we can notice this, we can make choices as to what to do about it, thus ameliorating any lessons of crisis.

When we participate in the lower consciousness level of mass humanity, we do not get such clear warning signals. Even though much of mass humanity's belief systems do not at all resonate with universal law, the sheer "weight" of so many engaging in negative beliefs makes it *feel like* the burden is not so great. The forceful magnetic field which is generated by a large number of people all participating in the same negative belief system in some ways buffers the effects of the dissonance that exists. There are still consequences, but in this case, we will not be able to read the warning signals. When consequences do come, we may be shocked, appalled and indignant because the flow of mass consciousness has put us to sleep.

We could list hundreds of universal laws; however many would be derivatives of others. Here we will delineate seven central laws.[11]

THE LAW OF ONE

The Unity and Interconnectedness of Existence

Everything is born of One Source, One Force, One Power, One Spirit, or any other name we give to what many call God, the creative, sustaining Force of the universe. This Force can be called The All, and the law is sometimes stated as: All Is One. The All is the essential element of everything; the way things appear through our five senses is the way the All manifests itself on the physical plane. This law is the first and most fundamental universal law. We have seen its resonance throughout the ages. We have seen it most strongly manifested in the Age of Cancer, yet have heard the essence of the law much more recently quoted by native Americans, Eastern philosophers and quantum physicists. The Law of One is an Aquarian mantra, as Aquarius wants us to recognize that the One Force is the essence of everything we know.

The Law of One says that we are birthed in the image of God and embody Divine characteristics. We are given the opportunity to evolve into more and more of an identification with our God-essence as we grow and change and become more self-aware. The extent to which we have evolved our consciousness can be measured by how much we allow our inner Power, our inner God, the One Force, to be manifested into our earthly life.

The Law of One provides us with great transformative power. Because everything is made of the same "stuff," because our essence is Spirit, as is the essence of everything we know, we have the ability to connect with and *transform the material world*, which will respond to directed, focused concentration of the same energy of which it is made. If we can learn to experience our commonality with everything in existence, if we can feel the resonance and the relationship between ourselves and everything else, we can be in a position to use that resonance to learn to transform what is around us. *We can then change our physical world to align with our desires.*

This sentence alone vividly illustrates the importance of attuning our desires with our heart, so that we are aligned with all universal law and cause no harm, injury or suffering. We already use our transformative power all the time without realizing it. To be able to *consciously and positively direct* our transformative power is a goal that is attainable with diligent practice, focused attention and a willingness to align with the Divine Force that fuels our every move.

Reading all of this, we may have an intellectual understanding of the Law of One. However, it is clear that this is not enough. To truly "get it," so that we can begin living as if it were true, to be able to connect with and exhibit such transformative power of which we are speaking, we need the *experience* of the All. An experience of the Law of One allows us to dissolve our separateness, the idea of ourselves as disconnected individuals, the idea of anything as an isolated entity. We go beyond our five senses and merge with the powerful rhythms of the universal Force, recognizing It as a mirror of who we really are.

As always, experiences can be translated into words, but never completely accurately. The descriptions serve as guides for what to expect and what direction to head, as they give us a general sense of what is possible. It seems that an intimate, focused prolonged connection with nature may grant the experience of the Law of One. Even one second of embodying this universal precept leaves us profoundly changed. When we recognize the inherent unity of existence, we recognize our connection with everything and everyone on the planet. We tap into our commonality and begin to understand that our thoughts, words and actions have implications for the universe. It is only when we experience this interconnectedness that we will be mature enough to create the global community that the Age of Aquarius urges us to do.

When the Law of One experience comes, our hearts are fully open, which allows us finally to merge the material world with that of Spirit, and we no longer experience any separation of ourselves from the inner essence and Divine power that permeates and radiates from everything we know. This was the goal of the Mystic archetype from the Age of Pisces, the age from which we are emerging — to synthesize the world of matter and the world of Spirit. The necessity of the open heart in this task is crucial. That is why ancient wisdom teaches that the closest we come to experiencing the All is when we experience the powerful state of being we call Love.

THE LAW OF CORRESPONDENCE

As Above, So Below

The Law of Correspondence is stated as: As above, so below; as below, so above. Whatever happens on the larger planes of existence is mirrored on the smaller planes. Conversely, what happens in the smaller worlds will be found in the larger worlds. Another way to say this is: What can be found in the macrocosm or larger universe, can be found in the microcosm or smaller universe, and vice-versa. According to this Law, a larger event such as a disaster in a foreign country has a corresponding connection with our smaller, more personal universes and the way we live our lives. Let us look at some simple examples that demonstrate this principle of correspondence.

If we draw a simple schematic of planets revolving around the sun, it would be largely indistinguishable from a schematic of electrons moving about the nucleus of an atom. From this simple model, we can deduce a connection of some sort between the solar system, the larger universe, and the structure of matter, the smaller universe. This correspondence is not an "accident," nor a "coincidence," but rather an example of how such synchronicity is inherent in the universe.

Here is another example. In 1913, the Danish physicist and Nobel laureate Niels Bohr developed a theory to illustrate how atoms are structured. He theorized that the electrons of the atom were arranged in different quantum levels, or shells, at different distances from the nucleus. Dr. Bohr postulated that the total number of shells is seven, the first shell holding two electrons, the second shell holding up to eight electrons and successive shells holding even more. This theory corresponds to the theory of the structure of the human energy field, or aura, the electromagnetic field which surrounds and interpenetrates the physical body. The energy field also has seven "shells," or levels, and, as in Bohr's electron shells, each successive level of the energy field holds increasingly complex energy patterns. The field itself is produced by the movement of energy through seven major energy centers, or chakras, spinning cones of energy, each containing a certain number of vortices. Once again, each successive energy center is constructed of more and more vortices.

Along the same lines, the ancient Egyptian and Greek Hermetic philosophers divided each of the three great planes of existence — the physical, mental and spiritual planes — into seven minor planes, with each of the minor planes divided once more into seven subplanes. Here again, each successive plane holds increasingly higher or more organized energies.

We find the Law of Correspondence inherent in any reflexology science which uses a small part of the body to diagnose or treat the entire body. In foot reflexology, for example, points on the foot correspond to different parts and organs of the physical body. Applying pressure to these points affects the corresponding organ or body part. Acupuncturists can treat the entire body by placing needles only in the outer ear. Some Eastern diagnostic techniques read disease or dysfunction in the entire body by evaluating characteristics of the facial features. Iridologists diagnose health patterns of the body by determining patterns in the iris of the eye.

Any synchronicity, or concurrence of larger and smaller events, is an example of the Law of Correspondence. Teacher, author and medical intuitive Dr. Caroline Myss points out the synchronicity between the economic state in the United States during the Depression, and the rise of the polio virus during the same period. She notes that as a nation we believed we were "crippled" by the economic depression which began in the 1920s and culminated in the 1929 Wall Street crash. During this time period, the polio virus, which crippled the human body, spread throughout the country. Right after World War II, when economically we were "back on our feet again," Salk created the polio vaccine and the virus was no longer the threat it had been.

What Dr. Myss makes clear is that the crippling of our nation's economy was mirrored physically in the epidemic caused by the polio virus. The emotional reaction to and the fear of our country's fragile economic state were also reflected in the growing hysteria about the invasion of the virus that caused poliomyelitis. Once the country was secure economically (the larger event), what was mirrored was the control of the polio virus and the eradication of the manifestation of the disease in individuals (the smaller event).

Interestingly enough, our President during this time period, Franklin D. Roosevelt, was stricken with the polio virus in 1921, the same year that the farm depression began. Roosevelt regarded the farm depression as the root cause of the economic collapse of the late 1920s.

In her teachings, Dr. Myss also points out that the fact that we have invented something as powerful as the atomic bomb should lead us to realize that the same power is available *inside of us*. According to the Law of Correspondence, we could not have created the atomic bomb were this not so. This interior power is, of course, the power the Aquarian Age will urge us to discover, manage and manifest.

How To Work with the Law of Correspondence

The Law of Correspondence holds tremendous potential for us because it helps us learn to evaluate events symbolically, to "read" universal messages in small events that are closer and more readily available to us than cosmic occurrences. Conversely, events in the outer world help us to become more aware of what is going on in the inner recesses of our psyche. Carl Jung, the father of psychoanalysis, stated:

> *Our psyche is set up in accord with the structure of the universe, and what happens in the macrocosm likewise happens in the infinitesimal and most subjective reaches of the psyche.* [12]

The English astronomer and mathematician Fred Hoyle says the same thing:

> *Our everyday experience even down to the smallest details seems to be so closely integrated to the grand scale features of the Universe that it is well nigh impossible to contemplate the two being separated.* [13]

Because all planes of existence mirror each other, events and occurrences on one plane can be used to solve problems on another. If it works "out there," it also works "in here." This means that the energy pattern of an event that occurs on a planetary level, such as a famine in one part of the globe, could also be found in the human body as a disease process, and will show up in the human psyche as distorted beliefs. There is actually one negative image, or distorted energetic configuration, linking all three levels. Psyche, physical body and planet are responding to one negative image which produces the same effects at different levels of existence. Working individually to transform our personal negative image is actually a very powerful way to solve a global problem. The solution begins with our own interior transformation.

For example, crisis in any country's political system can be read as mirroring the negativity in the country's consciousness, which is a result of negativity in each individual's consciousness. It is our responsibility, when we see turmoil in our own country, or in the world, to understand that the turmoil is a mirror for the turmoil in the mass consciousness. We must ask ourselves "Do I hold this same turmoil inside of me?" whether that turmoil is a lack of reverence, addictive behavior, dishonesty, greed or any other dissonant behavior. In this way, everything can teach us, everything can be an opportunity to become more self-aware so that we can evolve our consciousness. Everything can be guidance for what our next step should be.

Once again, we are referred to the first universal Law, the Law of One. Because we come from one Source, we are all connected, interrelated. The universe can be likened to an energy web or network. When we break through a level of consciousness to a higher level, we have put "medicine" into the energy network, and that medicine travels all over the globe. The more people that put medicine into the network, the stronger the medicine becomes, and the more it can affect healing.

THE LAW OF VIBRATION

A Dynamic Universe

This law says in essence: Everything moves; everything changes. The Law of Vibration is a principle of modern physics when physics describes the universe as having the attribute of dynamism — embodying activity, animation and change. This movement is inherent in the universe; it is to be expected. Thus, we can define life as incorporating change as the natural order of things. This makes evolution, and evolution of consciousness, as natural for the human being as breathing. When we refuse to move with the Law of Vibration, we immediately move out of harmony with life.

Ancient wisdom teaches, as does modern physics, that the varying appearances of matter on the earthly plane are due to varying rates of vibration. We can think of a continuum, with infinitely high vibrations at one point, and the lowest vibrations at a polar opposite point. In between we can place everything in existence, according to its vibratory rate, including thoughts, emotions and invisible forces (like radio waves), as well as concrete objects.

Raising Vibrations

Since all matter has a certain vibration, so too each individual has a certain vibratory rate. A physically, emotionally, mentally and spiritually healthy individual will manifest a specific vibratory rate. An ill or angry person will usually manifest a lower vibratory rate. To master the Law of Vibration, we must learn how to change our own vibratory rate when it is too low. When it is higher, we will feel better. In this way, because of our interconnected universe, we will also affect the vibratory rate of other people, material objects and the environment in general.

When we have the ability to change the vibrations of concrete objects, we change the way the object manifests itself on the earth dimension. Changing the outward manifestation of a concrete object by employing the Law of Vibration constitutes what we call a miracle, for example when Jesus of Nazareth turned water into wine at the Cana wedding feast. Changing the vibrations of our own energy field (the body of energetic configurations which surrounds and penetrates the human form) is not so daunting as performing what we think of as a miracle, and happens more than we realize.

When we raise the vibration of a low-vibrating energy field, or correct a dissonant vibration, we naturally feel better. A healthy vibration puts us more in tune with the universe, and life flows more easily and pleasurably. Raising and/or correcting our vibrational frequency can be accomplished by doing something as simple as taking a walk because moving the body physically naturally lifts the vibration to some degree. Eating food with a good strong vibration — freshly picked organic vegetables, for example — will likewise affect the vibration of our physical body. Blessing our food before we eat it, raises the food's vibration and thus ours when we ingest it. Saying a prayer, doing a good deed, opening our hearts, laughing, chanting a positive affirmation, appreciating a beautiful sunset — all these things raise or correct the vibratory rate of our energy field.

What is important to remember is that as we correct our vibration, we also effect the vibrations of the people and events around us. So, for example, if we are happy and laughing, our magnetics (the human energy field has an electromagnetic component to it) will pull others' fields into synchronicity with ours. The other person may resist this pull, of course, since we all have free will. However, our state of being has the potential to affect the state of being of others in very powerful ways.

This is the basic concept of laying-on-of-hands. The healer aligns as best she is able with the Divine energies of the One Force, allowing that energy to flow through her field freely. Acting as a conduit for this Divine Vibration, the healer then places her hands on the patient, and the patient's field is entrained to lift its vibration also. Since illness, pain, anxiety and the like have low vibrational rates, the lifting of the patient's vibration begins to transform distortions that exist in the energy field and can have a healing effect on disease.

When we learn to regulate our vibration, we regulate our moods, our thoughts, our lives. When we consciously choose to move with the higher vibrations rather than the lower ones, we are quite powerful. We are sending our higher vibrational energy through the universal energy web. One of our Aquarian lessons is to remember that how we hold our energy can have an enormous impact on our environment. It is time that we realized that events and people of low vibration do not have to pull us down, *no matter how large they are.* We can learn to hold a high vibration in the face of just about anything, with intention and focused concentration.

Dissolution

The glyph for Aquarius ♒ represents energy, and also is an alchemical symbol for dissolution. Dissolution is a transformation that allows us to slough off the lower vibrational energies and raise our vibration in order to change an outward manifestation. In raising our vibration, we actually *liberate* (here is another Aquarian word) higher vibrational energies that are always present within us, but trapped by the material form of our bodies. When these energies are liberated, they radiate from us, and we can begin to identify with the higher vibrations rather than the lower.

In the process of liberating the higher vibrational energies from the human energy field, any lower vibrational energies that stand in the way must also be let go of. This is what happens during a "healing crisis." We take in something (a supplement, an herb, high vibrational energy from a healer) that will entrain our energy to a higher level. Before we feel better from this, we may seem to get sick. What is really happening is that the lower vibrational energy is leaving the body, and as it does, we may exhibit the symptoms which that lower vibration holds in place, especially if we closely identify who we are with the lower vibrations.

For example, if we have always identified ourselves as being a victim, when the victim vibration is lifted out of the energy field, we feel the attraction that energy possesses for us and we hold onto it to some degree. Even though it is a low vibrational energy, we may treat it as a cherished possession, simply because it is familiar. The holding on allows the manifestation of whatever symptoms the victim vibration has brought into our lives, *including physical ones.* If the higher vibration which is forcing the victim vibration out of the field is strong enough, and if we really have the intention to let go of lower vibrational energy, the lower vibration will continue to move out even if we clutch at it. Once the lower vibrational energy is out of our system, the higher vibrations can be liberated and the desired effect achieved.

Consequences of Dissonance with the Law of Vibration

The Law of Vibration tells us that change is inherent in life, and we should expect it and cooperate with it. One of the consequences when we do not comply with the Law, when we do not allow change in our lives, can be illness. It is not the only reason that illness will develop, and not following the law certainly does not guarantee that we will get sick, but when we refuse to move, refuse to change, refuse to increase our consciousness, illness can be the result. Because every part of us has consciousness, so does every cell in our body. Our cells want to adhere to universal law, simply because it is the natural state of things. When we become frozen and we make a choice not to change, not to evolve, not to follow the natural pattern of the universe, we are in dissonance with the Law of Vibration. The dissonance, when protracted, blocks us from our longing to move with the great Power that is our essence. This can lower the vibratory rate of our cells, and illness can result.

Because Aquarius is so connected to energy and all its processes, the Aquarian Age will bring us the lessons and the information we need so that we can learn more about the potential of the Law of Vibration. As with each astrological age, the new age will implore us to move with the universal vibrational dance by embarking upon the quest for expanded consciousness.

THE LAW OF POLARITY

Relationship Between Opposites

The Law of Polarity states: Everything has its opposite, but these opposites are really two extreme poles on one continuum. There is a relationship between the opposites, and a dynamic balance can exist between them. There can be peaceful coexistence (here is Aquarian energy) between polarities.

The Kybalion, a treatise on Hermetic philosophy, states that opposites are identical in nature, but different in degree. In many cases, one pole seems positive, and the other negative, with the positive pole holding the higher vibration. It is a natural tendency to be drawn toward the positive, higher vibrational pole. An example of this would be the circular continuum which has love on one side and fear (which engenders hatred) on the other. The energy of love holds the higher vibration and we are naturally and instinctively drawn to this pole rather than the fear pole of low vibrational energy. It is only when our natural flow of energy becomes distorted that we are attracted to the lower vibration at the fear end of the continuum.

In other cases it is the middle of the continuum that holds the most organized, healthy energy. The continuum of hyperactivity and hypoactivity, for example, would be one in which the middle part of the continuum would be the most balanced.

The Principle of Polarity is evident in the world of physics. In 1930, a British physicist named Paul Dirac theorized that for every elementary particle (the name given to the smallest units of matter), there was another called an anti-particle. This led to the discovery, in 1932, by American physicist Carl Anderson, of the polar opposite of the electron, called the positron.

Electrons themselves have been found to simultaneously exhibit the characteristics of both particles and waves, previously thought to be two contradictory behaviors. Here we have the Law's potential for coexistence of opposites. In addition, because atomic particles are defined in terms of probability patterns, it cannot be stated whether a particle actually exists in a certain place, or does not. The atomic particle holds both the possibility of existence and the possibility of non-existence, at the same time, again creating relationship between polarities. Modern physics continues to uncover the coupling of what had previously been supposed to be non-relatable properties.

Lessons of the Law of Polarity were presented during the astrological Age of Gemini when humanity was asked to employ the attributes of Mercury, the Divine Messenger who could create relationship even between extremes. We can use the example of how traveling northward around the globe eventually becomes traveling southward to illustrate the Law of Polarity. North becomes south becomes north again; the opposites merge into each other. If we look at a continuum with black on one end and white on the other, we cannot point to one particular place and say that here is the exact spot when white becomes black. Everything is a matter of degree.

We use the Law of Polarity when we examine a zodiac sign's polar sign in order to understand the first sign more clearly. We see the manifestation of both the main sign and its polar opposite sign in events that occur during an astrological age. The polar opposite sign brings the initial sign much more into balance. Opposites can create quite a wonderful partnership, if both partners are willing to respect, and learn from, those energies in the other that they do not possess.

Transforming One Pole into the Other

The Law of Polarity coupled with the Law of Vibration gives us great transformative power. Because opposites belong to the same continuum, there exists a relationship between them, and *one pole can be transformed into what lies at the other end of the continuum.* We would automatically say, for example, that compassion and hatred are opposites, and indeed they are. However, if we have awareness of the Law of Polarity we also understand that because compassion and hatred are part of one continuum, the difference between them is a matter of degree, or we could say, vibration. We can think of instances in which compassion turned into hatred, or vice versa, or when the strong feeling of compassion at one end of the pole shifted to something that was near the middle of the continuum, with not nearly as much power or vibrancy.

The vibration of hatred in the human energy field is much different than that of compassion. Whereas compassion is a warm richly beautiful energy that flows smoothly from the fourth energy center, hatred is hard and blocks the natural energies which want to radiate from the heart. However, because both belong to the same continuum, it is possible to transform the vibration of hatred into compassion. In order to do this, one would have to know how to hold and radiate the vibration of compassion very strongly, without wavering at all, even in the face of someone very strongly holding the energy of hatred. We may have had the privilege to be in the company of someone whose heart was so open that just by being with them, our hard edges begin to melt and we are pulled along the compassion/hatred continuum toward the pole of compassion. If we practice holding the energy of compassion in order to become proficient at it, we begin to be able to access it more readily when we are in need of it. This would be either when we have been pulled away from the compassion pole to the other end of the continuum, or when we are in the presence of a person or persons who need their vibration raised so that they can move along the continuum toward the compassion energy.

We cannot transform something at one pole to something on another continuum. So, for example, hatred must be transformed into compassion, not courage or peace. However, once hatred is transformed into compassion, the magnetics of the energy will *harmonize* much more readily with other positive, high-vibrational energies, such as courage or serenity.

The idea of this kind of transformative power can give rise to all sorts of creative concepts about how to make the world a better place, an Aquarian quest. Once again, we begin to get the idea that it is the way that we hold our own energy — in other words, how we live our life — that is the position of power.

THE LAW OF RHYTHM

Compensating Movement

Rhythm can be found all around us — in music, in dance, in poetry, in the visual arts, in literature, in speech, in nature's biological and geophysical processes. It is defined as a flow characterized by some kind of regular recurrence. Words used to describe it, like cyclic, periodic and tidal, are similar to qualities associated with the moon, and indeed the moon's constant waxing and waning phases are an example of the Law of Rhythm in operation.

The Law of Rhythm tells us that everything has tides and cycles. It says that if the pendulum swings to the right, it will swing the same distance to the left. If there is expansion, there will be contraction. What rises will eventually fall. Every movement has a compensating movement, a returning flow, a counterbalancing action.

The Law of Rhythm operates between the two poles established by the Law of Polarity. This is not to say that the movement between the poles will go all the way to each extreme, but that any movement one way is counterbalanced by an equal movement in the other direction.

Let us look at the examples of this that we can find in nature. Day follows night follows day. The seasons recur. Plants grow, die, new seeds are planted, new plants grow and die. We sleep, then wake, then sleep again. The tide ebbs and flows. The moon waxes and wanes. The astrological ages flower, then dissipate. Cycle follows cycle.

Working with the Law of Rhythm

In our daily lives, we constantly experience the Law of Rhythm. We win, we lose. We cry, we laugh. We produce, we rest. We work, we play. We feast, we fast. We spend, we save. As we list all the movements between polarities, we can also become aware of what happens if the Law of Rhythm is thwarted by our human will. For example, if we feast, then fast, we stay in balance as far as our physical bodies are concerned. However, if we continue to feast, without remembering to have periods when we eat less, we grow fat. If we fast without ever feasting, we manifest the disease of anorexia. If we always move between the extremes of this continuum, we exhibit the disease of bulimia.

Or, if we work all the time, with no compensating rest period, we compromise our health and mental well-being and are termed a workaholic. If we never work and are always resting, we manifest laziness. If we cry all the time without ever laughing, we greatly lessen the quality of our lives. Likewise, if we laugh all the time, including during times when grief is more appropriate, we constrict the natural rhythm of our feelings, and keep ourselves from growing emotionally. The basis of bipolar disorder, a disease in which we lose contact with a healthy emotional rhythm, is when we continually swing from the extreme of outgoing, initiating active energy to the opposite pole of lethargy and non-movement.

Every movement has a compensating movement, and in order to move in harmony with the universe (and thereby make life a lot smoother), we need to be aware of any time we willfully stop the balancing movement in the other direction. The compensating movement bestows a state of equilibrium, of balance, of poise. If we are not feeling these qualities in our lives, we need to look at places where a balancing movement is lacking. For example, if we find ourselves always irritated because we seem to be constantly taking care of everyone all the time, we need to put the same amount of energy into caring for ourselves. Then the irritation will disappear. What is dangerous is when we repress the irritation or anger we feel when we do not balance our actions. In these cases, the negative feelings usually end up in our cell tissue and our physical health is compromised. Overdoing in any area is unhealthy. However, that does not mean that we cannot have occasional intense periods of activity. We just need to remember to balance them with a compensating movement. We also need to remember that to continually swing between two extremes is very unhealthy. We need to balance any extremes with periods of smaller movements toward the center of the continuum.

With different situations, there will be different lengths of time between the rhythmical movements. For example, the moon waxes for two weeks, then wanes for two weeks. Summer and winter solstice are six months apart. Our inhalations and exhalations follow each other in time periods of seconds. The astrological ages take over two thousand years for the rhythmic cycle to move. Ancient wisdom teaches that some cycles are not repeated in one lifetime; in that case, the compensating movement might not occur for several lifetimes. So we must be aware that our life span may not encompass enough linear time in order to experience or notice the rhythmic flow of certain events.

The Law of Rhythm and Emotions

The Law of Rhythm applies as well to our experience of emotions. Ancient wisdom holds that our capacity for feeling what we call "positive" emotions is balanced with our capacity for feeling what we call "negative" emotions. If we are able to feel great joy and happiness, then so too, we are able to feel great sorrow and grief. It is put forth by the ancient wisdom philosophies that in the matter of experiencing emotions, the negative will precede the positive. So it is through our deepening ability to feel painful emotions that our capacity for joyful emotions is increased.

Even though the Law of Rhythm says that the pendulum must swing, even along a continuum such as the compassion/hatred one, as we become more conscious, we can learn to recognize when the swing is headed toward the negative emotional pole. At that point, we learn to raise our vibration so that we are lifted "above" the negative emotion and do not become immersed in it, nor participate in it. We use our will to direct our energy back toward the positive pole and "pull" ourselves in that direction. Even when we have practiced bringing out our compassion so that we have a magnificent heart, there may be times when the pendulum begins to swing toward the hatred end of the continuum. This is an opportunity to strengthen the heart even more. We say no to the temptation to live in and act from fear and hatred, even though our pendulum swing offers us the chance to do so.

THE LAW OF CAUSE AND EFFECT

A Chain of Causes

The Kybalion states the Law of Cause and Effect as follows: "Every Cause has its Effect; every Effect has its Cause; everything happens according to Law; Chance is but a name for Law not recognized."[14] This means that nothing happens arbitrarily; everything that happens is ruled by universal law, and every event can be reduced to its simplest terms as being a manifestation of universal law in action. The event itself can be defined by either being in harmony or in dissonance with universal law.

It is easy to understand cause and effect: it is part of Newtonian physics, and we see it working around us every day. We heat water, it boils. We drop glass on a hard floor, it shatters. We eat some food, our hunger is assuaged. We turn the key in the car ignition, the car starts. We neglect to put fuel in the car, it does not run. We can look at any event, and know that behind the effect there is a cause.

Ancient wisdom takes this farther and says that behind every event there is a chain of causes. We can begin to understand this concept by seeing that the leap from eating food to satisfying our hunger is not one step, but rather many having to do with the process of digestion.

Likewise, we can follow the chain of events back even farther, to find the cause of why we were hungry at that certain time in the first place. Turning the key in the car ignition is not the only step to the car starting; there is a mechanical sequence in between which is part of the chain of causes. In addition, the car started because we turned the key in the ignition, but what was our catalyst to do so? Where were we going? What motivated our action? The effect is actually the end point of a long chain of causes, each linked with each other.

Let us take the example of something we might ordinarily call "chance" — the pulling of one card out of a deck of cards. The causes of pulling a certain card out of the deck are many. It would depend upon how the deck of cards was handled, shuffled and cut, the order of the cards when the deck was picked up, the stickiness of the fingers of the card puller, and the physical force exerted as the card was grasped.

According to the world of energy, the pulling of a card would also depend upon things that may not be readily apparent, like the invisible forces of energetic configurations representing our thought patterns and belief systems. Now we must also consider questions like: What was the frame of mind of the card puller? Was the card puller attempting to pull a high or low card? Did the card puller believe that she was able to intuitively pull the card she wished? What was the energy around the card puller at the time of the action? What were the thought patterns of the card puller a second before the card was selected? How did these energetic configurations of the card puller affect the pulling of the card?

As we can see, cause and effect become more complex. If we begin to think about everything in terms of energy, we see that the "random" act of pulling a card from a deck is actually the result of the way that many energy patterns intermingle with each other. Changing one energetic configuration in the picture can result in a different outcome. In addition, there is no starting point. Every cause is preceded by another cause, and we could follow this chain back endlessly. And so *The Kybalion* states, with regard to the Law of Cause and Effect: "There is a relation existing between everything that has gone before, and everything that follows." Everything we do, think, feel and say is part of a chain of causes that will produce an effect.

Choices as Causes

When we look at our lives, we can know that what we see is an effect that has been preceded by many causes. We can also know that the causes are created by choices we continually make. So, for example, a woman looks at her house and says that the place where she lives is not the place she "would have chosen," that it does not resonate with her, is not really where she would like to be living. If she is able to truthfully follow the chain of events which led to her being in these surroundings, she might tell a story like the following. "I chose to marry someone who liked to spend a lot of money. I knew this about him, but decided to ignore it, even though it bothered me, and I linked my finances with his anyway. We both worked hard, but he spent the money as soon as it came in. I allowed him to convince me not to put money aside for necessaries. Even though this brought me much anxiety, I preferred anxiety to speaking out about what was happening because I was more worried about creating discord between us. I have never liked or been able to confront anyone, especially those close to me. Soon we could not pay the mortgage and our house went into foreclosure. After that we had to declare bankruptcy. Then we had a child, which took more money. He has never changed his spending habits, I have never changed my inability to speak up and assert myself, and now I am much too scared to think about making a major life change. So we are living in this house that is too small and dark and does not feel good at all."

We can see the places where the woman had options, where she could have made other choices that would have produced a different ending. We can also see that she allowed her anxieties and fears to make the choices for her. She is responsible for creating her life, and she permitted her fears to play a major role in that creation. Thus, the end result is not to her liking.

The woman's truthful statements are ones which show a lot of self-awareness, something which would probably not come to us right away, or easily. Her first story might have been one of blaming her husband for her predicament, without seeing that she also made choices along the way that created the effect she disliked. For her to create a different ending, she must realize that her life is not created by someone else without her permission. Giving up control over our lives is another choice we make. In order to have a different outcome from what is present, we have to take the risk to make different choices. The only place we can begin to do that is in the present moment. What we choose *today*, creates our tomorrow.

The Law of Karma

The concept that everything we do, say, think, and feel is part of a great chain which results in certain effects is also the concept of karma, the idea that what we sow, we must reap, whether from this lifetime, or past lifetimes. Many people hold an incorrect definition of karma, thinking of it as something absolute, the consequences for the sum total of our actions from which we cannot escape. While it is true that we cannot erase our karma, it is also true that *we can modify its effects upon us by our present actions.*

Karma means "action" and we do reap the effect from all our past actions, as well as past thoughts and feelings. Every cause in the chain of causes that precedes an effect can be thought of as a seed sown. The end result, the effect, is the plant that grows from those seeds. If the seeds that are sown are distorted in any way, so too is the plant that grows from them in some way distorted. If we look around us at our lives and see things that we do not like, we can be sure that somehow, some way, we have planted seeds to create the very object of our discontent.

In one sense, we must live with this, enduring the ramifications of what we have sown previously. However, the meaning of "action" which is assigned to karma, incorporates the idea that action in the present moment can be a mitigating force with regard to our karma. This means that what we do today, right now, will effect our lives tomorrow. And what we do today, right now, with regard to the karma which is already present, can also change the energy of the karmic conditions.

Let us look at an example. A man builds a house that clearly falls short of proper construction. He does this in order to save money, time and the energy which the proper construction would require. The house looks okay on the outside, but structurally it is not sound. This, however, suits the man fine, and he moves in.

For one year he lives in this house with seemingly no problems. The house is not falling down, and the man is able to live without fixing the little things that have broken. It would seem that there are no consequences for his shortcuts. However, one day a storm is forecast to move through the area. As it gets closer, the storm upgrades to a hurricane. The man knows that his house is not structured to withstand hurricane force winds.

At this point, several things can happen. The man may stay in the house during the storm and be injured or even die as the house collapses around him. This could be seen as an example of the man reaping what he sowed. However, the man has other options. He may decide that he will leave the house to escape injury. Now his "karma" has changed and, although the man loses his house and its possessions, injury to his physical body is not part of his fate.

The man may also decide to take as many valuables as possible with him when he leaves. Gathering what he can into his car, he drives to a shelter and remains there for the duration of the storm. Now his karma has shifted once again. He is not destitute at the end of the storm.

When he goes back to his house after the hurricane has passed, he decides to salvage some of the debris in order to use it to rebuild. He also collects broken pieces of china and pottery to give to his brother, who is an artist who will use them to create something new. As he sifts through the rubble of his karma, the man realizes how he misdirected his energies in building the house, and vows to construct his next house with more foresight and responsible choices. Now his karma is much different than the first scenario in which he lost everything, including his physical safety. Now he has his health, some possessions, building materials to begin his new house, a supply of objects to give to his artist brother, and most importantly, a new perspective about short-term and long-term consequences of spending time and money.

The point being made here is that, although the Law of Karma, a derivative of the Law of Cause and Effect, cannot be made to disappear, we can take action to ensure that we overcome as much negativity from past thoughts and deeds as possible. Instead of whining and complaining about how unfair life is, we accept our present circumstances as what is, we see how our past actions and thoughts contributed to creating the circumstances and we endeavor to work as much as possible to change what we previously sowed, so that today we sow a different kind of seed that will blossom into a different plant tomorrow. *Our point of power is in the moment.* It is right now, today, not tomorrow, not next week. We can modify the effects of past causes by what action we take this minute.

The Creative Process

One of our purposes in the universe is to continually create, just as the Divine Force continually creates, and we are to use our creative potential as fully as possible. To create means to engage in the everyday process by which we continually make choices (create causes) toward an end goal (a desired effect). As we evolve, we wake up more and more to the realization that we constantly create our lives; life does not just "happen" to us. This concept is not one which is readily understood and integrated; we have not been educated by, nor immersed in, a society that holds the belief that we can consciously create our lives, something that is bound to change as the Aquarian Age advances. We also hold *unconscious* goals based on our negative belief systems, such as the desire to remain a victim, and so many of our choices support negative goals of which we are not aware. The evolutionary process includes increasing our self-awareness in order to unearth such negative beliefs. This allows us to use the Law of Cause and Effect for the creation of a happier life.

The idea of creating our lives gives us tremendous freedom, and simultaneously, tremendous responsibility. The ability to *consciously* direct our lives to be created in accordance with our heart's desires and soul's longing, are lessons demanded by the Aquarian Age. A further section, called "The Creative Process," explores in detail how to actively create a life we love.

THE LAW OF GENDER

Masculine and Feminine Energy

One way that we can begin to allow our creative power to emerge is by understanding the Law of Gender. The Law of Gender states a simple concept: Everything contains both masculine and feminine energy. In every person, thing and event we can find masculine as well as feminine qualities. These qualities are not to be confused with the popular application of the words masculine and feminine which denote a person's biological and/or sexual presentation. The Law of Gender refers to the energetic qualities of masculinity and femininity. These forces are strongly attracted to each other, and each has a magnetic pull on the other. Any attraction/repulsion dynamic is an illustration of the Law of Gender at work.

In physics, the Law of Gender is apparent in something called the nuclear force, which is an extraordinarily strong interaction that holds atomic nuclei together. It is also evident in gravitation, and in the fact that positively charged particles and negatively charged particles attract each other.

When we put everything within a framework of energy, we can clearly define specific masculine and feminine elements. When used in tandem, these seemingly opposite, but actually complementary, energies (here is the Law of Polarity) allow for the full expression of our creative power. In order to utilize our creative potential, we must employ both our masculine and feminine energy. Let us look at the job of each, always keeping in mind that we inherently have the ability to express *both* masculine and feminine energy, no matter which one is our biological or sexual presentation in this lifetime.

Masculine energy initiates, selects, directs, points, concentrates, transmits, gives out, distributes, commands, orders, expresses, exhibits, displays and presents. All of these qualities are also associated with the will. In western society, many of these qualities are associated with, and are the expected behavior for, members of the male gender. Unfortunately, the expression of the masculine qualities is often to the exclusion of the feminine properties.

The job of the feminine energy is to receive and appreciate the masculine energy and from that energy the feminine begins a process of generating, multiplying, developing, augmenting, extending, intensifying, enlarging, expanding, ripening and giving birth to. The feminine energy is also related to the emotions, rather than the will. Again, society tends to polarize the feminine qualities in a woman to the exclusion of the complementary masculine properties.

The description of masculine and feminine energy together includes the qualities which constitute a healthy individual. One of the lessons from the Age of Aries was to balance our internal masculine and feminine energy in such a way that allows us to live life to the fullest. It will be in the Aquarian Age that society truly recognizes this; as it does, our belief systems, behavior and social structures will change accordingly.

When we fully utilize our creative potential, we naturally employ both masculine and feminine energy. Here is how it works. The spark of illumination which begins the creative process is neither masculine nor feminine, but comes from the One Divine Force. It is the job of the masculine energy to grasp that spark and initiate the creative process. The masculine energy then directs the spark to the feminine energy, which receives and develops it, and finally gives birth to something which manifests the Divine spark in our own individual way on the earthly plane.

Consequences of Undeveloped Masculine Energy

We need to have our masculine and feminine energy working together as a team. When one or the other is not developed fully, there are negative consequences. When we have not developed our internal masculine energies, we are unable to grasp the Divine spark for ourselves. We lack the aggressiveness that is needed to reach out and grasp what we want.

When this happens, we use instead the masculine energy of someone else, or of a group, and allow it to initiate and direct for us. *The Kybalion* states that those who have highly developed masculine energies are the people whom we call charismatic or magnetic. Their will is developed in such a way that it can serve to be the initiating force for others whose own will is not fully developed.

Here is a metaphor for what happens when masculine energy is undeveloped. We sit at a dinner table laden with every kind of food. We know which food we desire, but we lack the initiative to reach out and take it, so we let someone else choose for us and put food on our plate. Are we happy with what is being served to us? Maybe, maybe not. What is apparent, however, is that we have no choice in the food we are being served and expected to eat. The meal may be to our liking today, but we cannot guarantee the same results tomorrow, and there is sure to come a time when we are served food that we do not like at all.

Or, we want to build a house, but lack the masculine energy needed to initiate the process. So we allow the plans to be drawn up by someone else, for example, our family of origin. Our parents and siblings have a fine time deciding what is needed, what rooms will go where, what sizes they will be, what style of architecture; we, however, have no say in the matter. We are then given the plans and no matter how they do not fit with what we would have liked, we use our feminine energy to expand upon them in an attempt to "make them our own." However, the house that is finally built is not what would have been constructed had we had the plans drawn up to our specifications.

Having weak masculine energy, we still go through life creating. It is just that what we give birth to can be likened to a reproduction of someone else's original painting. Masculine energy is necessary to select the spark of an idea, point it and transmit it to the feminine energy. This is also the definition of what our will does — selecting and directing energy. Without this force of internal selection and direction, we are forced to take what is handed to us, since we are not setting in motion any energy of our own. A person in whom masculine energy is lax or weak complains about his or her lack of will and will power. Because, with undeveloped masculine energy, the ideas that we expand upon via our feminine energy are not truly our own, what we create is not aligned with *our* desires, but with the desires of others, and we will not be truly satisfied with what we have created.

Let us look at a real life situation in which this distortion manifests. A woman desires to own her own business. However, she has not been taught to express her masculine energy, since it was not appropriate to do so within the structure of her original family. Her parents held the belief that not only should a woman be secondary to a man in the business world, but that qualities like aggression, initiative and directing ability were not to be expressed by a female. The family's belief system conformed to societal belief systems at the time the woman was growing up, so the magnetics of its pull on the woman were very strong, and consequently, her masculine energy was never developed. Now, as an adult, this is still the case.

Because she did not develop masculine energy, does not mean that the woman does not have the ability to be aggressive, initiating or directive, but that these qualities are like weak muscles in her energetic makeup and she will not easily manifest them. So although she really longs to start her own business, she is afraid to reach out for the things that would initiate her ideas and would set her desires in motion. What is more readily at her disposal are the sparks of Divine Force which have been used to create her family's belief system regarding what is appropriate for a woman in business. (Remember that any Divine spark from the One Force can be used to create positively, as well as negatively or distortedly.) Since the woman does not know how to grasp the

Divine spark herself, she uses what her family has already grasped and gives birth to something that is totally unsatisfactory with regard to her own desires and longing. This manifests as a job as a secretary in the kind of business she herself would like to run.

In order for the woman to create her desire, she must master how to upwell and manifest her masculine energy. This is a learning process she must go through. It may be started by her dissatisfaction at not having her own business. The discomfort of that may be the impetus that starts her on a journey of self-discovery and transformation that will allow her to have what she wants. Here again is how pain and discomfort urge us to move into places where we otherwise might not go, in order to become more powerful, more satisfied, happier individuals with our creative power at our disposal.

What the woman must do in order to create according to her own desires is to stop the habit of allowing her family or society to direct her energy for her. This is the journey out of mass consciousness, when we individuate from the group and stop using group belief systems which do not resonate with us.

If we do not develop our masculine qualities, we will be forever tied to the masculine energy of a person, or group of people, who will provide that energy and consequently, the directing power of our will, for us.

Consequences of Distorted Feminine Energy

Another thing that happens which can distort the creative process is when our feminine energy is undeveloped, or we have a habit of using it for someone or ones other than ourselves. In the first instance, we may have a lot of ideas, but no "womb" in which they can grow, develop and finally be manifested via the birthing process. In this case the ideas are never brought to fruition. This would manifest as a person who has much creative potential and lots of great ideas, but that potential never amounts to anything. The strong impetus at the beginning of a project dwindles and fizzles out because there is no "vessel" in which it can be nurtured and grown to maturity.

The second instance is all too familiar in our society, especially for women. Because feminine energy also has to do with a feeling mode (rather than the will mode of masculine energy), an expression of femininity naturally enables a person to be more in touch with their emotions. However, when men are taught not to develop their feminine sides, they lack the ability to process feelings that they have. Every human being has feelings and emotions, some of them strong, whether the person is in touch with those feelings and able to name them or not. When a person needs to process emotions and does not know how, a woman sometimes volunteers to process the emotions for the other person. Unfortunately this behavior can be erroneously defined as being "nurturing."

The feminine energy *is* nurturing; this is one of the qualities of the feminine. However, sometimes, women especially, will use their nurturing qualities and their "creative wombs" in service of someone else's need to feel, rather than for their own creative birthing process and the emotions that naturally accompany that act. This can affect the health of their reproductive organs. It is the responsibility of each person to develop his or her own masculine and feminine energy so that the will and emotion can be used in a balanced, healthy way.

Here is an example. A woman desires to focus her attention on increasing her skills in oil painting with the hope of making it a career. Her masculine energy has grasped this idea and initiates it, directing the woman to begin to set up a studio in which she can work. The resources and time are available, and the woman is very excited about what she is about to create.

However, at the same time, the woman's husband begins to have problems with his boss at work. He has very real and legitimate feelings of being dishonored, disrespected and undervalued. The husband has not developed his feminine energy enough to deal with the discomfort of having these feelings and so, in an effort to stop feeling them, he suppresses them, which manifests in a mild depression.

If the woman's feminine energy is healthily developed, she continues her own creative process of setting up a studio, while she is also being supportive of her husband. This means that, although she is willing to listen and talk about her husband's situation with him, and is empathetic to the fact that he is having difficulty allowing his feelings to come forth, she also insists that her husband take responsibility for processing his feelings, even though he may not be very good at it. At all times, she is a partner to her husband as he goes through this difficult period, while realizing that he ultimately must cross his emotional thresholds by himself; she cannot do it for him. She is able to continue with her own plans, and not let the creative spark that has been grasped by her masculine energy wither and die.

If, however, the woman has been taught that her creative feminine energy is always to be used in service of another first, instead of herself, she turns away from what her masculine energy is directing toward her feminine with regard to her painting studio. She engages in the idea that she must take care of and nurture her husband, and "fix" his situation, at expense to herself. She throws all her feminine energy into caretaking and nurturing her husband and his feelings because he does not know, and has never had to learn, how to do that for himself. The woman applies the feminine qualities of generating, developing, augmenting and ripening to her husband's predicament. She attempts to solve his problem, and takes on his responsibility to feel and work with his feelings.

Energetically, the woman has actually taken her husband's low vibrational energy into her energy field, where she knows how to process it and raise its vibration. She feels the burden of this; her husband feels better. His load is lightened, while his wife has to work at dissipating and transforming his low vibrational energy that she is now carrying. Because her feminine energy goes into that task, it is detoured from giving birth to her original desire which was to create a painting studio and paint in it. By the time she has raised her vibration back to normal (and this could take days, weeks or months depending on how proficient the woman is at transforming her own energy), her enthusiasm (or masculine energy connected with the project) has also dissolved. When the masculine energy is left hanging with no feminine to receive it or be attracted to it, it loses its impetus. The woman is left with resentment and anger because her desire has been thwarted, not by her husband, but by her own compliance with allowing her feminine energy to be used for someone else's needs before hers.

Sometimes a couple will habitually use each other's masculine or feminine energy in a similar way. If the man lacks the ability to use his feminine energy, he will count on the woman for that energy. Conversely, the woman, lacking masculine energy, will depend on the man to supply that. This kind of an arrangement may actually work well for a while. The challenge is to learn from the other person, so that we can become more proficient in handling our own interior energies. If we do not do this, somewhere along the road in our evolutionary development, we will come up against a time when the fact that we do not have access to both our interior masculine and feminine energy is too painful to tolerate. At this point, we are forced to create an interior balance.

We obviously need our masculine and feminine working together to express our creative power. In the Age of Aries, when the masculine energy came charging into Taurean femininity, humanity was presented with the possibility of creating something powerful. This is the potential revealed by the true partnership of Venus and Mars, and it is available to all of us.

ENERGY LITERACY

THE AGE OF ENERGY

As we move more fully into the Aquarian Age, we are going to be asked to reframe our idea of how the universe works into an energy-based model. In other words, we will need to become "energy literate." The new age will demand of us that we have a concept of life as an energetic, rather than a mechanical, reality. This means that we must begin to incorporate the understanding of the unity and interconnectedness implicit throughout life, giving up our ideas of ourselves and our world as being "constituted of separately existing fragments."[15] We will need to transform the Piscean Age/Newtonian physics descriptions of fragmented life that have become obsolete in the face of evolution of consciousness and discoveries in modern physics.

As we transform our belief systems of how life works into ones in which energy is the basis of reality, we will naturally begin to integrate philosophies of ancient wisdom and the words of the mystics as well as the cutting edge science of the Aquarian Age. When we combine our knowledge of physics with universal law and metaphysical truth, we come up with some basic guidelines for understanding how the world, as energy, works. This is a glimmer of the physics/metaphysics marriage that will give us a new model for understanding and interpreting our universe.

Energy obeys universal law. By honing in on certain aspects of the law, we can delineate common energy patterns that are present in daily life. In order to make the leap into the paradigm of the new age, it is helpful to have an everyday energy "primer" which gives us more detailed knowledge of the nature and properties of energy, in addition to the ways in which such a paradigm impacts our lives.

The following energetic precepts are extrapolated from universal law. They can be found in ancient wisdom, Eastern and Western mystical philosophy, the work of current pioneers in the domain of energy/Spirit awareness and the continually mind-blowing arena of modern quantum physics and atomic theory.

THE NATURE OF ENERGY

Energy Is Spirit

When we are reminded that energy is Spirit (remember, Spirit is a synonym for God, Divine Force, Divine Light, etc.), we are repeating the first lesson of the Universe — the Law of One. We have learned that Spirit is everywhere, is the matrix on which all matter is formed. When we study the properties of energy, we can get a better understanding of Spirit and how it works, because it is easy to see parallels between the two. Both energy and Spirit are invisible forces, neither of which observes the time-space barriers of linear consciousness. Both energy and Spirit exhibit the qualities of unity, interconnectedness and dynamism. A true understanding of Spirit is an *experience* of it; it is too broad and deep a concept to ever be defined by our linear vocabulary. However, as we come to know energy better and how energy works, we come to a better knowledge of Spirit and how Spirit can work.

When hands-on-healers "run energy" from the infinite sea of universal energy through themselves and into the patient, they are also "running Spirit" into the patient, increasing the patient's awareness of him or herself at the level of Spirit. For the healer, there is no separation of the notion of energy from the notion of Spirit; they are one and the same.

When modern physics tells us to think of everything as energy, we can translate that directive into thinking of everything as Spirit. Thus, we engage in the practicum assigned by the Age of Aquarius, which is to find Divine Essence in everything, simply as a matter of fact. Our goal is to automatically see and hear and feel Spirit in every part of existence. Once this concept is integrated, the rods and cones of our eyes (those areas being ruled by Aquarius) will shift physiologically so that we will more easily be able to actually *see* Spirit as energy waves, vibrations and/or colors in objects, people and events around us. It is postulated that as infants and very young children, we naturally have this kind of sight which we lose as we begin to accept the general belief that extrasensory vision is not possible. In believing that we cannot see Spirit/energy, we send messages to our eyes and they grow accordingly. As society transforms its beliefs about reality, to include the belief that Spirit/energy imbues all of existence and is able to be perceived by human sight, we will not have to lose our ability for this kind of sight perception.

To get more of a sense of the concept that energy is merely a way that Spirit shows up in the physical dimension, it can be helpful to interchange the words "energy" and "Spirit" in the rest of this section.

Spirit/Energy Is a Living, All-Pervasive Force

We can start to integrate the complex theories of relativity and quantum physics by thinking of everything as "made of" energy. Both the groups that we call organic (animal, plant) and inorganic (mineral, man-made), as well as those invisible things like air, breath, thoughts, emotions, radio waves, holograms, auras, magnetism, gravity and consciousness are energy. The energies of which everything is made emerge out of One Source, and are constantly changing and connecting with each other.

In defining matter as energy, we shatter the illusion that matter is inert. According to modern physics, the "dense" matter of concrete objects is actually a collection of packets of energy with space in between the packets, the space and the energy packets making up the substance. In quantum physics these energy packets can be defined only in terms of patterns of probability of interconnectedness . No more solid building blocks of matter, just energy and how it will relate to other energy as it emerges from the whole.

Whether a concrete object or an invisible force, the fact remains that energy, like Spirit, is pervasive throughout existence. Whatever we can name is energy. Whatever we can name is Spirit.

Let us take this concept about matter being energy, and modern physics' definition of energy's three main properties, and use them to re-define human beings. A definition of *human beings as energy* would read as follows.

> *All human beings come from the same Source. It is to be expected that humans will change and evolve. Their lives are shaped according to how they relate and connect with each other.*

Now let us make these statements more personal. Read these aloud.

> *I come from the same Source as everyone else. My goal in life is to change and evolve. My life is shaped according to how I relate and connect with everyone else.*

These are Aquarian statements and they essentially sum up a new philosophy for living that will emerge from the Aquarian Age.

All Experiences Hold Spiritual/Energetic Directives

The challenge of being in a body and living on planet earth is to remember our Spirit natures in spite of the density of form. If we are awake to it, Spirit continually sends us messages about how to live gracefully on this planet. Spirit is a wise teacher and there is never a time when we are without Its guidance. Spirit's directives can always be read in the world all around us. Events are energy, and energy is Spirit. Spirit carries with It all the wisdom we need to live a life of joy and ease. Were we wise enough to decode it, we could get spiritual guidance from anywhere — from the physical activities of our cells to the positions of the planets, from the health of our bodies to the state of current events, from the migration patterns of birds to the probability patterns of sub-atomic particles. There is no place is our universe where the message of Spirit cannot be read.

Sometimes we do not want to hear or read any spiritual guidance because we know that in order to follow it, we would have to change our lives. Change is a big anxiety-producer. Even though intellectually we may be able to discern that certain changes in our lives would be beneficial, when it comes down to making them, our inner dragons rear up and keep us right where we are. We hold onto the familiar because it *is* familiar, even when we know it does not really fit our lives and where we want to go and who we want to be.

Sometimes we become so mired in a situation, we are not aware that we have the power of choice to change our circumstances; we buy into an illusion that we are "stuck" and have no choices available, especial-ly if we cannot imagine a solution. Our linear minds can give us a mil-lion reasons why we must avoid change and support the status quo.

When we get caught in these traps, Spirit is always there to help us remember the Law of Vibration which says that change is an inherent element of life and that to resist change puts us in dissonance with the Universe. Spirit gets our attention by creating what we pay attention to the most — pain, crisis, illness, trauma, discomfort, a loss of control. Spurred by a desire to alleviate our pain, we begin a journey of trans-formation, a journey we might not set out on were there no crisis in our lives.

Our crisis is handed to us because it contains the most perfect, per-sonalized opportunities for us to learn how to become more intimate with our own Spirit natures. Each crisis, small or large, is a hero's jour-ney from which we can emerge stronger, wiser and more aware that who we *really* are cannot be defined solely by the material world, but has to do with a Force much more magnificent than what we had imagined. It is difficult to remember, when we are in crisis and just want our pain to go away and not come back, that we are embarking upon a hero's journey. However, if at some point we are able to say to Spirit, "*I am willing* to be guided through this; *I am willing* to be transformed by my pain," our burdens can lighten a great deal. In any crisis, our spiritual assistance is as strong as it can be, *no matter what the appearance of the situation is from the outside.*

Crisis is an energetic pattern, and it comes into our lives for different reasons at different times. Sometimes it is just about becoming stronger and more able to open our hearts. Sometimes it is because we have agreed to model courage or love, while under fire, so that the rest of the world can receive the gift of seeing this model and thus can more easily learn to embody the same qualities of Spirit themselves. Sometimes crisis is something we agreed to go through before we came into the body because we were aware that the hero's journey would quickly put us in touch with our powerful Spirit natures. This does not make moving through the crisis any easier. Even Jesus of Nazareth, in the Gethsemane garden, felt the burden of the next step of his journey.

But many times pain, crisis and illness are like warning signals that it is time to get on our horse, get in line to receive our magical sword and shield and set off to discover something new about ourselves. When we ignore the warning signs, the form and intensity of the crisis necessary to move us, increases. Thorwald Dethlefsen and Rudiger Dahlke, in their book, *The Healing Power of Illness*, give a great metaphor for this.[16] They say that ignoring our physical symptoms of discomfort is like taking our car to the mechanic because a red warning light has come on on the dashboard. "Fix this," we say, "I don't want to see this warning light." When we arrive several hours later, the mechanic says to us, "Your problem is solved. The warning light is off." "Great!" we say. "What did you do?" The mechanic replies, "I disconnected the warning light."

We can disconnect the warning lights in our lives, but the problem that caused the lights to go on in the first place will still be there. Rather than stick our heads in the sand, it might be wise to use the discomfort in our lives to do some exploration. We will find that every single discomfort, every single pain and crisis is encoded with energetic/spiritual directives that help reorient our lives for the better. We need to keep remembering that another name for Spirit is the Will-to-Good, the Force that has our very best interests as its focus.

The new Aquarian Age will bring with it the unfolding wisdom to hone our ability to translate the meaning of events and situations to uncover the daily living guidance within the events. In the section on spiritual translation, we explore some specifics of how to enter into and move through this process.

PROPERTIES OF ENERGY

Energetic Pathways Create an Energy Net

Because energy wants to connect, it creates passageways and paths between and among people, things and events. From the enclosed environment of a cell in our body, to the healthy flow patterns of energy throughout the human energy field, to universal cosmic transmissions, energy follows specific roadways as it fulfills its longing to create relationships. Chief Seattle intuitively knew of this facet of the universe when he spoke of the web that connected all people. The Internet provides us with a clear-cut metaphor for this aspect of energy and also allows us to see how instantaneously these connections are made. As on the Internet, time and space are no obstacles to energy's desire for interconnectedness.

Let us keep in mind the image of a universe in which there are prescribed routes on which energy travels, connecting one thing to all things, one person to all people, one event to all events, and people, things and events to each other. All this culminates in a richly complex tapestry of energetic pathways that ultimately encompass all of existence.

Because of this interwoven aspect of life, any change in one part of the energy net has ramifications for the whole net. In this way, our thoughts, words and deeds, all of which are energy and all of which send out a certain vibration which travels through the energy net, are extremely important and powerful as they eventually affect the entire universe. The next thought we have, the next words we speak, the next action we undertake, will have an effect on the entire world. These effects are felt most strongly in those close to us — our family and friends — but eventually, they permeate the entire universal web.

Energy Organizes Itself in Fields

When we think of objects as energy, the first place where we need to widen our perception is in thinking that the object stops at the edges of its physical boundaries. Energetically, the definition of an object does not stop with its physical form. The energy of an object penetrates the physical form and also surrounds the form.

Just as humans tend to live in communities, energy also organizes itself in "communities" called energy fields. Every person has an energy field. Every object, those we call living as well as those we call non-living, has an energy field. Every event has an energy field. The energy field is a region around, and including, the object, person or event; it surrounds and penetrates the form or the situation. The field holds the template (matrix or model) for the way the object or event will manifest. This means that the field *precedes* the physical form of the object and precedes the way an event will manifest. The energy field comes first, then the form or physical presentation follows the patterns set up in the energy field.[17]

The fact that the energy field precedes the form of an object has magnificent implication. If we can learn to regulate and order an energy field, we can affect physical form, including the body's manifestations of physical disease. In the human being, the energy field holds the templates for the four levels delineated by the holistic model; that is, the physical, the emotional, the mental and the spiritual. So, by working with the human energy field, we have access to the patterns that hold in place any distortions on any of the four levels, and we find that a distortion on one level is linked to a distortion on other levels. (The next section, "The Synergistic Community of the Human Energy Field," explores the human energy field further and explains how distortions come to be in the energy field in the first place.)

There already has been, and continues to be, pioneering work carried on, many times at major universities throughout the world, to explore the ramifications of developing the human potential to work with energy fields in such a manner. As the Aquarian Age energies grow stronger, schools which teach the philosophy and techniques of energy healing become more proliferate. Meanwhile, the technology that will give us a clear and definitive picture of the energy field has yet to be developed. Methods such as Kirlian photography are able to produce only crude representations of a field. It is possible to "view" the energy field quite specifically on an intuitive level; however, to do so with consistent clarity demands that the viewer be consciously and responsibly self-aware. As the Age of Aquarius gains momentum, it is inevitable that the area of energy fields will be more deeply explored, and this exploration will be the underlayment not only for new technology, but also for paradigm shifts in the way we view life.

Energy Fields Can Interpenetrate Other Energy Fields

One of the properties of energy is that energy of different frequencies can occupy the same place at the same time. We can examine this in the context of the human energy field, which normally extends outward from our physical body approximately three feet in all directions.

Whenever someone comes closer than three feet to us, our energy field and the other person's interpenetrate. This can feel comfortable, uncomfortable or neutral, depending upon the structure of each person's field. For example, if the field of someone who dislikes strong feelings is interpenetrated by someone who is very angry, the first person will feel very uncomfortable, and maybe even frightened, by the interpenetration, even if the angry person is not actively exhibiting their angry mood.

When a stranger or someone we do not know well steps into our personal, energetic "space," that is, the three-foot radius of our field around the body, again, it can feel very uncomfortable. When we are in a crowded situation, we may unconsciously strengthen the outer boundary of our field at the same time that we pull our field inward, decreasing the radius to perhaps a foot, or even less, around our body to preserve our personal space. If the outer boundary of our field is very strong, it does not invite anyone to move into our field, and most people will intuitively "read" that message and not invade our space, physically, emotionally or mentally. If our boundary is very permeable, it is like an open door, inviting another's energy to come in.

Once another's energy does interpenetrate ours, it can mix and harmonize with our energy in a pleasing way, or clash and conflict with our field in an irritating way. Another's energy in our field may encourage our field to take on different flow patterns and vibrational rates, even if we would not consciously choose those flow patterns and vibrational rates ourselves. In other words, our field can be coerced into taking on configurations, whether positive or negative, suggested by the field of another person or group of people. This is how we engage in mass consciousness; if everyone is doing it, it is much easier to go along than to choose a different behavior. Likewise, recovery support groups like Alcoholics Anonymous offer positive energy configurations to replace negative ones that represent inappropriate and unhealthy behavior. What is actually happening is that we are allowing the magnetics of a stronger will to supercede our own will, and begin directing our energy for us. In any case, when outside energy is in our field, we sense what is happening, either consciously or unconsciously, and we respond according to our habitual energetic patterns that grow out of our belief systems.

If we are spiritually and psychologically strong and healthy, we say "No" to unpleasant or uncomfortable energy that comes knocking on our door. However, if we are under stress, our healthy "No" response may be weakened. Or, if we hold a belief system (which will show up as an energetic configuration in our field) which says that we do not have the power or the right to say "No," we open up our field to allow negative energy in.[18]

Energy Is Magnetic

Every energy field has a magnetic aspect to it. In this sense, the field behaves in the way we expect magnetism to work, as either attracting or repulsing other energy fields. It is important to realize that our own human energy fields constantly exhibit this property and attract certain people or situations into our lives.

Every belief system that we hold manifests as an energetic configuration in our energy field. So, for example, the negative belief "Life is a burden" will show up in different ways in the energy in and around the body. There will be specific distorted arrangements of energy in our field which are based on this belief system. This one statement will influence how full of energy our field is and what energetic pathways are mapped throughout the field. It will determine if and how we block communication between certain parts of the field. It will also affect the vibrational level of our field as well as the way the field is "structured" as a vessel for holding our energy. Certain areas of the field will hold distortions of these factors more strongly than others.

All of these conditions influence the magnetics of our field, and our magnetics determines the kind of energy we attract into our life. Basically, we attract energy that corresponds with our belief systems. So if we believe "I always end up with friends who betray me," we might as well wear a sign that says, "Only betrayers are welcome in my life." By energizing the negative belief, by thinking it, voicing it, complaining about it, worrying about it and using it to define who we are, we are setting up the magnetics of our field to attract the betrayers!

We attract what we believe we deserve to attract. We attract according to how we define ourselves. If we hold certain attitudes towards life, we attract specific attitudes that will go hand in hand with ours. If we believe we are a victim, we will attract the perpetrator. If we live the role of the lost lamb, we will attract the savior. If we think and act as the child, we will attract the parent. If we need to be the tyrant, we will attract the one who agrees to being tyrannized, and so on. Our energy fields send out "radio waves" announcing exactly who we think we are. These frequencies hold the magnetics to attract into our lives those people who will play the role we need so that we have the opportunity to realize what beliefs we hold. Once we realize how we are "programmed" with certain negative belief systems, we can make choices to either maintain the status quo, or transform negative beliefs into something that will serve us better.

We will only attract according to our consciousness. Each of us has areas of life where we are more evolved than in other areas. We may be very consciously astute about the way we run our business, but not so consciously astute about the way we engage in an intimate relationship. In our business life, we attract highly evolved thinkers and planners, good employees, responsible suppliers; however our love life is full of potholes and crises as we attract only those who will collude with our negative beliefs about how relationships work.

It is easy to see that a first step toward having healthy magnetics is to be aware of what belief systems we hold. Our statements about how we believe life works for us are of paramount importance, because essentially, these statements are setting up the magnetics of our field and running our lives. We must define the belief system that we want to transform before the transformation can begin.

Energy Tells Us the Truth about a Situation

The energetic reality of a person or event is sometimes quite different from its outward manifestation. What something looks like from the outside does not always equate with the truth of the situation. External appearances can belie what is really happening, hence the saying "Appearances can be deceiving." How many times have we smiled or spoken sweetly to someone when in actuality we were quite perturbed with the person? How many times have we sensed that something was going on beneath the surface of what was being said or acted out, in spite of appearances to the contrary — for example, someone's relationship which superficially looked great, but actually was falling apart?

One of the perks in being able to read energy is that is gives us the true picture of what is happening. If we interpret things energetically, we get the truth, because distortions will show up as such in the energy field. An undistorted field will have a certain structure, a certain vibratory rate, a certain flow or movement pattern of energy, and a certain optimum amount of energy moving through it. These factors will of course vary, depending on what field we are sensing or observing. When we "read" an energy field, we see the truth about how energy is being held — where it is flowing and not flowing, what the vibratory rate is, what patterns are distorted, where the structure is inadequate — and all these things translate into what is really going on. For example, a person who is insincerely saying "I love you" in order to manipulate us, will manifest that insincerity in his or her field. The energy around the person's heart area, which emanates the quality of love, will be depleted rather than full and radiating out beautifully, while the back of the body between the shoulder blades and up toward the shoulders will have too much energy twisting in distorted patterns.

The human energy field will also manifest a disease process before it shows up in the body. The person may look and even feel okay at the moment, but the energy field, because it is the mold into which the physical body fits, will show the beginning of the disease process, many times as a mental and emotional distortion which then "trickles down" into the physical body.

Beneath what things look like on the surface, there exists another world which includes many stories. When viewing ourselves from the energetic level we can sense energetic configurations which represent everything that has ever happened to us during our life so far. In addition to our own story, our energy will include, to some degree, the story of our family of origin, and that of all our ancestors. Our energy contains structures describing our karma (the consequences of all past action) and to some degree the karma of our family and our ancestors which is called the inherited tribal karma. Our energy also holds configurations representing our connection to our life task (the reason we chose to incarnate), as well as resonances from the family's group life task. All of our energetic configurations, and the strength they have, will present a picture of our fears, our defenses, our clarity of thought, our emotional maturity and our state of health. Our energetic makeup shows how much Spirit we allow to come through us.

So when we look at someone and assess the person based on external factors, like appearance, career, residence and financial status, we get a very incomplete picture. There is an encyclopedia of information upon which we are not even touching. As we begin to understand life from an energetic perspective, we begin to evaluate people and events on an entirely different level.

We must keep in mind that if we do not learn to quiet the chatter of our linear minds, we will do poorly at any attempt to sense energy. We cannot get rid of our linear minds, and certainly do not want to. But at certain times we can get the linear mind out of the driver's seat and put it in the back seat as a passenger. We can exercise our muscles of concentration and focus. In this way we begin to open to energetic dimensions where time and space are irrelevant, and wisdom is continually and obviously available.

OUR RELATIONSHIP
WITH ENERGY

We Can Direct Energy

As human beings, we have an innate ability to direct energy, and this is something we do every day. We direct energy simply by focusing our attention on something. We are directing energy when we pay attention to an action, a person, a thought, a feeling, a world event, and so on.

Directing energy can be likened to shooting an arrow, with whatever we are paying attention to as the target. We focus on the target and send an arrow of our energy toward it. If we simply shoot arrows without having a clearly defined target, we are shooting wastefully and in vain. It is of utmost importance to have clearly delineated a goal at which we are directing our energy. "What is it that I want?" is a question that must be specifically and carefully answered before we bother fitting the arrow to the bowstring.

The action of directing energy, or focusing attention, is regulated by our will. The will corrals our energy, gives it its assignment, and sends it toward a target. This corresponds to the job of the masculine energy which we described in the Law of Gender. If we do not decide ourselves where we want our arrows to go, if we do not shoot our own arrows, someone else will gladly take our quiver of arrows and direct them for us. However, someone else will direct our arrows toward a goal of her own, not a goal that we have decided upon, and it is very likely that we will not be thrilled with the results.

We also direct energy at specific people whenever we think about them, whether those thoughts are positive ones or negative ones. Whenever we have a thought with someone's name in it, we are "e-mailing" that person energetically. It is like shooting an arrow of our energy to the person. Because energy does not observe the normal linear time-space barriers that we are used to, this energy sending can be done instantaneously even over distances, just like the way the Internet works. We can send energy to anyone, anywhere and this can be done as quickly as our thoughts proceed.

Here is an example. A woman sees the back of a man from across a room, and something about the way he is standing and the wave of his hair attracts her attention. She begins to wonder about who he is and stares intently at his back. Within one minute, the man turns around and, even though the room is crowded, he immediately looks directly at the woman. Without realizing what was happening energetically, the woman's focus on the man and her concentration in wondering about him was so strong that she actually sent out a streamer, or ribbon, of energy from her field. This energy streamer first brushed, and then interpenetrated, the man's field. The man turned around because he felt this, just as he would feel a tap on the shoulder. He intuitively followed the energy streamer to its source and looked directly at the women.

We can send energy with more consciously focused intention, such as when we pray for someone. Again, the connection with the other person is established simply by bringing that person to mind. The intention of prayer gives the person an energy boost, flooding the person's field with the high vibrational energy that prayer carries. A deluge of high vibrational energy will increase something called "coherence" in the recipient's field, bringing more order to it. In this case, order means a higher vibrational level, a fullness of energy, healthier flow patterns and a well-structured vessel to hold the energy. This can manifest in the recipient's life as many things, such as an easing of something which was previously considered a burden, the ability to have an insight which guides the person through a troubled time or simply a feeling of being loved.

Sending a prayer to people increases the flow of Spirit through their beings, and increases their ability to flow with Spirit, thereby make their lives easier in some way. When we pray for a group of people, such as flood or fire victims, we send healthy, loving energy to the entire group. When we pray for resolution of a conflict, near at home or far away, we send supportive, loving energy to the energy field that surrounds the conflict.

Just as we can send prayer, or good thoughts, we can conversely send negative thoughts. Negative energy can damage another's field, especially if it is sent on the prongs of a strong emotion such as anger or hatred. Even what we may consider to be "harmless" negative thoughts or actions send a bad vibration into and through the energy net. Again, if we link the negative thought with the name of a person, we are sending a harmful arrow of energy to that person.

When we link the name of a person with a negative thought or statement, we must remember the Law of Karma; what we give out, we are destined to reap one way or the other. This is universal law. Also, when we send energy to another, we create a bond or energetic cord with that person. So if we send love, we enjoy the pleasure of an energetic love cord between ourselves and another, and through this cord feelings of love can travel back and forth, to the benefit of both people.

However, if we send hateful energy, we create a bond or cord through which hateful energy can travel back and forth, and so the sender must share in any hateful thought that the recipient creates. We may not realize that when we dislike someone and think about how much we dislike them and what their faults are on a regular basis, it is like we are tying ourselves to that other person, which is exactly what we say we do not want to do. By stopping our negative thoughts of others, we release the cords that bind us, and the energy previously used to sustain any negative cords can come back into our lives for our use and pleasure.

Additionally, the energy of any thought, word or deed is sent via the energy net, so its vibrations are eventually shared with everyone. We may not realize this because we see things from a very narrow perspective. However, if we were able to take our blinders off and step back and see the whole picture, we might be astounded and upset at where the energy of our negative thoughts travels. Energetically, it is a fact that negative energy sent to someone we see as an "enemy" will, via the energy net, also eventually send negativity to those we love and back to us.

Consciously directing our energy is one of the most important things that we can do because without direction, we cannot hit the target we want to energize. When we energize a target enough, we are able to bring that target into our lives on the physical plane. Without self-direction of our energy, we let life happen to us, rather than creating what we want. We will explore the ability to direct energy more fully in the section on the creative process.

Our Thoughts Have an Impact

It is sometimes difficult to remember that, energetically, things that do not have a visible, concrete form *are just as real and can have the same impact as the concrete.* If we throw a rock at a window, the window may break. If we direct a thought of a certain negative vibration at another person, the thought can also have a shattering effect, not only on the person at whom it was thrown, but, because of life's interconnectedness, eventually also on the thrower and ultimately on all of existence. Because they can cause such energetic chaos, it is important to reiterate this concept that our thoughts, however fleeting, can do damage.

Let me give an example that made me understand the concept of what impact the energy of thoughts can have. I was driving my car on one of the narrow bridges that straddle the small creeks in my neighborhood, when three young bicyclists came riding toward me. They were all about ten years old, and two were riding their bikes on the correct side of the road, but the other was riding on the left side, which meant she had to pass right by my car. The bridge was narrow to begin with, and because the child was riding on the wrong side of the road, I had to slow down to a snail's pace. I was in a hurry and this irritated me, and in the space of a few seconds, I thought: "What a stupid child. She is not even wearing a helmet. What is wrong with her, and what is wrong with her parents that they are not teaching her the safety rules of bicycling?"

I probably never would have even remembered this incident, the thoughts came so quickly, and as quickly left as soon as I passed the children. However, that night, I had a dream in which I was shown the impact of my thoughts not only on the child herself, but on her family. I was shown the energetic burden the child was already carrying from her family, in which there had been drug use and death; I was shown, literally and viscerally, how my irreverent, thoughtless thoughts added to the child's burden and also made it more difficult for her family to break out of their negative patterns. Such is the power of the web of life: when we are all connected, our negativity, as well as our grace, travels as quickly as information on the Internet.

Because of its effect upon me, this dream was one of the most powerful that I have ever had. I was forced to take responsibility for what I had done, and was shown ways in which I could make amends. It was difficult and painful to take responsibility for those careless thoughts, but the images of the dream so clearly showed me the additional pain I had caused that there was no question in my mind that taking responsibility was the only direction in which I wanted to move. That simple act of taking responsibility for our thoughts is a very necessary step if we want to reach for higher consciousness, and it will have profound results. Needless to say, from the moment of that dream, I have been more aware of the power of my thoughts, and more careful about them, even though that is not always easy.

Another area in which we can see the power of the energy of our thoughts is the health of our bodies. The new science of psychoneuro-immunology is the scientific way to say "body/mind connection." This is the way in which the mind and its thoughts influence the physical health of the body. Scientists like Dr. Candace Pert are finding themselves having to declare that the body is continually eavesdropping on our thoughts. And it does not stop there; the body takes what we think and runs with it, ultimately creating our health or disease. There is a shift in the energy field every time we entertain a thought, either in a positive or negative direction, and repetitious energetic shifts eventually impact the physical body.

An interesting experiment is to keep track of the body or health vocabulary we habitually use when speaking. Phrases and statements like, "a pain in the neck," "This is killing me," or "I just cannot stand up for myself" all impact our body in a negative way. When we use such language, we need to be aware that we do so at our own expense.

Conversely, positive images and statements are medicine for what ails us. Simply holding a positive image for a few seconds begins to shift the energy field into more healthy configurations. Remember this: when we have a negative image or thought, we need to remedy it immediately with a positive image. Then we have neutralized the situation. In order to begin to actually bring the positive image into our life, we must "dose" ourselves with its medicine many more times than we engage in taking in the toxins of the negative image.

We Are Affected by the Vibrational Rate of Other Energy Fields

Energy naturally flows from a higher vibrational source to a lower vibrational source. A person's energy field can resonate at a lower-than-healthy vibrational rate for several reasons: trauma, lack of sleep, stress, illness, environmental toxins, drug and alcohol use and poor diet are a few. If a person with a low vibrational field connects in some way with a person whose field has a higher vibration, the person with the higher vibrational field will begin to send energy to the person with the lower vibration. Higher vibration does not always mean "better." A strong negative emotion can, for example, rev up the vibration of our field, but there will be some very distorted and dangerous configurations that can be transferred to the field of another person, if that person lacks the ability to set a strong boundary against the negative configurations.

It is our responsibility to recognize when we are depleted energetically. This will feel like being physically depleted, emotionally and mentally fatigued, stressed or burned-out. In that case, if we wish to send energy to someone else, we had better take care of ourselves first. Otherwise we will do ourselves and the other person no good, and may allow a negative configuration from another's field to gain a foothold in our field. If this happens, once we charge up our field and reestablish a healthy flow, we usually can automatically move the negative configuration out of our field and replace it with our own positive configurations based on healthy belief systems.

It is important for us to become aware of the vibrational levels around us, and how those vibratory rates are affecting us. We are intuitively aware when we walk into a room, what vibration it carries and if it is comfortable for us to stay in that vibration. A room can hold the vibration of the people who were in it previously, even though the people are no longer there. The stronger the emotions which have been released in a room, the longer the energy of those emotions stays in the room itself. This is true for most environments. Not only emotions affect the vibratory rate of an environment. Any kind of energetic release will affect the vibration: thoughtforms, prayer, good intentions, bad intentions, as well as the radiation of electromagnetic fields. For example, because of its electromagnetic field, fluorescent lighting will affect the vibration of a room to a point where it can begin to negatively affect us after a certain amount of time.

If we are immersed in a field with an unhealthy vibratory rate, after a certain amount of time it will begin to have some effect upon our energy field, *unless we have consciously learned to hold our own vibratory rate at a healthy level.* This ability comes with practice, and there is no shortcut for learning it. To hold a healthy vibratory rate very strongly is a vital proficiency necessary for anyone who hopes to be a leader for humanity as we enter the new Aquarian Age.

Certain physical environments will recharge our field and lift our vibratory level. This can be a natural outdoor environment or a room in which we habitually instill a healthy vibrational rate. There are many places on our beautiful planet which still emit tremendously strong healing vibrations, such as the redwood forests along the western coast of the United States. This is why native American cultures would send a person "to the earth" if his or her "spirit was sick." Many times lying on the earth, swimming in a body of salt water or even pressing our body against a tree will naturally align our energy field and adjust our vibratory rate to a healthy level.

Other ways to adjust our vibratory rate are laughing, smiling, thinking of someone we love with whom we have a healthy relationship, physical activity, meditating, being with a pet, playing with a baby or young child, listening to certain music, looking at certain colors,[19] chanting, and thousands of other ways. It is important that we know which "remedy" is available and works the best for us when we need a boost.

We Can Read Energy

We quite naturally read energy all the time, although we may not be aware that we use this ability. We get cues which aid us in reading energy from our physical body, our instinctual awareness, high sensory perception and our intuition. Using one or more of these sensing devices, we interpret energy patterns that impact our own field.

Physiological sensations are the way our body tells us when we are in either a compatible or non-compatible energetic environment. If we have uncomfortable sensation in our body, however vague, we need to pay attention to it because it is trying to tell us something. The more we tune into our bodies and allow ourselves to *experience* our physical sensations, the more aware we will be as to how we are responding to the energy which is interacting with our own energy field. We can actually become quite skilled at interpreting physical sensations that let us know our body is trying to tell us something. For example, one of my clients found that she always experienced a certain tightening sensation in her solar plexus when someone was lying to her. Another person realized that he became "fuzzy-headed" when in the presence of someone who was very passively angry, that is, angry and expressing it in subtle ways that did not resemble an active angry outburst.

Sometimes our first sensor in reading energy is not our body, but a more primitive feeling that something is okay or not okay. In this case we are using our instinctual awareness to check out energy that is impacting us. Our instinctual awareness allows us to read energy that impacts our safety and the safety of those we love. This "read" happens very quickly and we usually respond without a conscious linear thought process. We have energetic feelers for this purpose that are constantly evaluating our environment.

Most people's high sensory perception is not well developed. This kind of perception involves using any of the five senses to read energy. High sensory sight would mean that we actually "see" energy fields — as colors, configurations and moving patterns. High sensory hearing can allow us to recognize health or distortion in people, places or events by "hearing" certain sounds or tones. High sensory smell like-wise gives us information about energy patterns by matching them with a certain aroma. If our sense of taste is high sensory, we experi-ence specific tastes that correspond with various energy patterns. With high sensory touch, we would get a kinesthetic sensation of the energy field we are exploring.

Our intuitive perception is one of our most refined energy-reading tools. Many times it comes to us via a lightning-like flash of insight. Suddenly, we simply know something to be true, no matter what infor-mation outer circumstances may be relaying. Other times, we get "pieces" of an intuitive puzzle we are trying to solve. Over time, we fit the pieces together and attain insightful perception of a situation.

Many times we consciously seek to awaken our intuition by quiet-ing our linear mind. Our minds and our intuition share the same "office space" of our sixth energy center, or third eye. (See the next section, "The Synergistic Community of the Human Energy Field," for more specific information about the sixth energy center.) Because the linear mind tends to be noisy, clattering about with an agenda and a lot of activity, it usually ends up hogging most of the sixth energy center's office space; our intuition is relegated to a small corner. Then we won-der why our intuition is not stronger. For intuition to be heard, it must become just as weighty a tenant in the sixth energy center as our linear mind function. Practices such as meditation allow this to happen.

When we finally still the linear mind and allow our intuition equal office space, we get the insights we need. These insights will often come in the form of principles, rather than specific answers or solutions; that is one way we know that we are onto something.[20] If we get a solution without understanding the principle behind it, we have farther to go. The integration of a spiritual principle allows us to use it any time we need to energetically read a situation and solve a problem with similar resonances.

THE SYNERGISTIC
COMMUNITY OF THE
HUMAN ENERGY FIELD

THE HUMAN ENERGY FIELD

The Energy Field As Our Life Story

We carry our life story with us at all times. We carry the historical facts, as well as the way that we have interpreted the facts. The flavor of our interpretation of our past experiences is interwoven into our present experiences; through these eyes we define what happens to us and subsequently respond or react to what we experience.

Suppose we have been victimized in the past. It is possible that we will carry the victim motif forward and use it to define everything that happens to us. In fact, we can come to expect to be victimized, and we will become adept at defining all the angles and facets of our experiences from the viewpoint of victimization. We can become quite capable of finding victim energy, even when it is not there! In doing so, we create it. The work of self-awareness and evolving consciousness allows us to disconnect from this victim perspective of life and helps us to find the ways in which we have grown stronger from our wounds. This last piece is transformational work (which is explored more fully in the last section, "Gathering the Gifts") that allows us to stand our past, no matter what negativity it includes, on its head and view it from an entirely different perspective.

Before any transformational work can occur, we need to be aware of just what it is that we want to transform. We need to know the themes we continually carry with us that thread themselves throughout our interpretation of our life experiences. These themes can be found as energetic configurations in the field of energy that surrounds and penetrates our physical body. This field of energy is called the aura, or the human energy field. Our health — physically, mentally, emotionally and spiritually — is affected by the habitual energetic configurations in our energy field.

The terrain of energy called the human energy field chronicles our life, both past and present. It contains the schematics of our belief systems. In it is written our personal saga of our adventure on this planet. It includes the templates for the physical body, everything to do with our feelings, all our mental thoughtforms and our ability to contact the God Force. These are the four levels of our being — physical, emotional, mental and spiritual. In the energy field, these four levels, although able to be perceived separately, are unalterably intermixed. They are like ingredients that go into making a cake. Just as we cannot adequately describe a cake by calling it simply "eggs" or simply "flour," we cannot adequately describe a human being by naming any less than all four levels.

The Energy Field As a Vehicle for Divinity

DIVINE
LIGHT
✩

The main purpose of the human energy field is to be a vehicle to carry Divine Light and to radiate It out to the environment. The field is specifically designed for this purpose. The work of becoming more self-aware increases our field's ability to carry the Divine Light Force. As we do this work, we feel more connected to a Greater Force which allows us to feel safe and secure; we feel more connected to a Light which brings pleasure into our lives, as well as the ability to love and to feel loved. We may increase our capacity for holding Light in small increments, or in leaps and bounds; the speed with which we hone our ability to carry Divinity really does not matter, as long as we hold the intention to move forward.

At a basic level, when we look at the human energy field, we look for the ways in which the field is able to carry Light, and the ways in which it blocks the Light from being carried. The blocks are defenses birthed from negative beliefs; they are filled with our fears and insecurities. They manifest as places in the energy field where we do not allow energy to move, or we detour it from healthy flow patterns. We may keep the vibration of the energy lower than what is necessary for our overall health, or we may not allow enough energy in a certain part of the field. The blocks in our field will eventually affect the physical body; at the same time, they will be played out as patterns in our lives that cause us discomfort and pain. However, the good news about the energy field is that it is transformational ground; at all times we have the ability to affect the ambience it broadcasts.

Although we may not be able to see the energy field with the eyes of the clairvoyant, we can be aware of its structure and organization by paying attention to those parts of our lives that are difficult and those parts that are easy. We pay attention to the stories that we tell and the statements that we repeat, realizing that these stories and statements are encoded with beliefs, both positive and negative, which steer our lives on a certain course. Our beliefs also have a profound effect upon the physical body. The beliefs we hold either foster and support the health of the energy field and physical body, or undermine it, and they are represented in the energy field by specific configurations.

How Our Negative Beliefs Are Formed

We adopt our belief systems in two ways. We may simply accept the beliefs handed to us by our families, by society or by any group that has some authority over us. These beliefs are usually introduced into our psyches when we are children and they are subsequently encoded in us energetically. Since everything is energy — our belief systems as well as every part of our body — the beliefs penetrate and actually become part of the energetic configurations in our cell tissue.

We also create our beliefs based on our experiences and the way we interpret them. A "bad" experience leads to a negative belief.

Something happens that hurts us, and we deduce that this is how life is. We may form a belief based on one single experience that lasts for one second, or on experiences that are repeated over and over. Again, these beliefs become energetically encoded in the physical body itself.

When a belief system is formed, it is manifested in the energy field by a certain energetic configuration that either supports or undermines the health of the energy field. The field is healthy when it has appropriate movement that follows certain flow patterns, when it has a certain vibrational level and when it is full of energy. By not allowing certain movement and flow, by keeping the vibrational level low and the quantity of energy less than full, we prevent ourselves from feeling painful experiences and energizing their accompanying thoughtforms. We construct highly efficient barriers that block movement, fullness and vibrancy of the field in order not to feel pain. These barriers are defense mechanisms which actually protect the negative belief system and keep us from evaluating it or looking at it closely. The energetic configuration of our pain becomes a frightening internal dragon and we spend a lot of energy trying to make believe it is not there.

When we create defense mechanisms, it is because we want to protect ourselves. Especially as children, these devices may be absolutely necessary in order for us to survive — physically, mentally, emotionally and spiritually. It is important to remember that our defenses are set into place as a loving gesture of protection at a time when we are experiencing fear and pain. Because we have defenses and the subsequent energy field distortions they create, does not mean we are bad. It means we are human!

Everyone has defenses and it is the challenge of the human condition to dismantle them. As we mature, we outgrow the need for our defenses, but by then they have become so habitual that they feel like they are part of who we are. We usually do not even realize that we have these defenses, until we focus our attention specifically in order to investigate them.

The defense mechanisms hinder the health of the field and thus the health of our lives. If we can detect a negative belief system, we can unearth the defense mechanisms it spawns. We can pinpoint the energetic configurations that hamper the health of the energy field and explore these "energy monsters" which actually detract from our lives more than protect us. The dismantling of a negative configuration is a hero's journey of facing our fears and that which we previously thought would destroy us. It is the journey of the evolved warrior-of-the-heart who seeks the Castle of Light. We come to realize that the Castle is our energy field — our body, our mind, our feelings, and the Spirit we have been created to hold.

Structure *of the Human Energy Field*

The human energy field is a body of basically electro-magnetic energy, which penetrates the physical body and normally extends around it to a distance of about three feet. The field can be retracted in closer to the body, and also infinitely expanded. The field is actually created by the whirling motion of energy centers, located at various points on the body. These energy centers (called chakras in the Hindu texts) can be thought of as intake-outake valves for energy; they take in energy from the universal field of energy which exists all around us, and also can release energy into the universal field. Another good analogy for these energy centers is as multi-tasked computers that contain programs built on our belief systems. There are seven major energy centers with points located on the physical body. There are also three centers located above the head; we will become familiar with these during the Aquarian Age. In addition, there are numerous minor energy centers located at specific points on the body.[21]

The energy centers appear as cones of energy, with the tip of the cone inserting into specific places on the body. The second through the sixth centers are paired; for each energy cone that inserts into the front of the body, there is a corresponding cone of energy inserting into the spinal column. The tips of these cones of energy "plug into" a power current that runs from the seventh energy center at the top of the head, to the first center between the legs. We call the cones of energy on the front of the body the front aspects; the ones along the spine are called the back aspects.

Each of the seven major energy centers nourishes specific parts of the body, both organs and systems. Each center plays a specific role in processing everything we experience, either producing the definition of the experience, or an emotion accompanying it or an opinion about it and so forth. Each of the seven major centers is also programmed to deal with belief systems about specific issues. Every belief system is associated with one of the seven major energy centers, and the positive or negative aspect of the belief system affects the health of the part of the body with which that energy center is associated.

The energy field holds the templates for the four levels of the human being — the physical, emotional, mental and spiritual. Dysfunction in any one level will affect the other levels. Because the energy field precedes the body, disease will show up in the field before it manifests physically. It is possible to prevent physical disease by clearing the emotional, mental and spiritual levels of the field before their distortion impacts the physical level of the body.

If we had the technology to give us an accurate visible picture of our energy field, we could look at it and interpret the energetic configurations as either being healthy or not healthy. Subsequently, we could then surmise which organs and systems of the body were at risk because of negative belief systems. Since we do not have such technology available to us at the moment, we must pay close attention to our beliefs and recognize the negative ones. By doing so, we can accurately predict which parts of our physical bodies are being compromised by our habitual negative beliefs.

The Energy Field As Community

In studying the energy field, it is helpful to divide the body into seven sections, each of which is nourished by one of the seven major energy centers. Each of these seven sections contains specific organs and body systems. Each of the seven sections has relationships with the other sections. These relationships vary in strength and character, but no section is isolated from another. For the health of the human being, a certain communication, balance, harmony and working partnership must exist among the seven sections. The whole energy field is like a synergistic community; when the synergy is disturbed, so is the life of the person. *Figure A* shows the seven sections and the specific parts of the body supported by each energy center.

The energy center for each of the seven body sections is like a computer program that deals with certain psychological issues. If we look deeply, we can find correspondences between the psychological issues and specific parts of the body. For example, the area governed by the first energy center regulates the immune system; correspondingly, the first center deals with issues of safety and security, just as our immune system does. Again, the relationships among the seven areas of the body is important. If, for example, our sense of safety is lacking in the first center, there is no way that the second center, which deals with our perception of how powerful we are, can be healthy.

Additionally, each center is associated with what are esoterically called the seven sacred planets (the sun and moon being included as planets). When we explore some of the mythological stories that are attributed to the gods and goddesses associated with these planets, we can understand each center a little more. Once again, synergistic relationships must exist among these internal deities for our life to be healthy.

When we understand the body in terms of energy, and understand the programming of psychological issues which is carried on by each energy center, we move into the realm of the new science of psycho-neuroimmunology, another way to say soul-mind-body connection. We begin to understand the part we play in creating the health of the body, and the health of our overall lives. Understanding the body as energy, we also begin to realize the potential of the life force available in every single cell.

Remember that we can substitute the word "Spirit" for the word "energy." Recognizing the body as Spirit-based, we grow out of having our awareness about our body focused merely in the physical plane. The human body is a marvelous, miraculous, living, synergistic, community-minded structure which manifests the God-Force that is alive in every one of our cells; understanding ourselves in terms of the human energy field only serves to underline that miracle.

Disease As a Hero's Journey

As we study connections between negative beliefs and the health of our lives and bodies, let us remember that when we manifest pain or disease, we have not done "something wrong." We are merely participating in life as it tends to work on this planet. The question to ask when we are sick or in pain is not "What did I do wrong?" or "Why is this happening?" but rather "This is what is. What do I want to do with it? What is the hero's journey I am about to embark upon?"

Viewing disease as an initiatory process in the organic evolution of our consciousness casts us in the role of warriors of the heart, rather than inept humans who have made terrible mistakes that we now have to pay for. Let us behold disease and crisis with respect and honor for the person who has just received a steed, a sword and a shield, and under the auspices of a Great Force, is off to find the Castle of Light and the treasure within.

FIGURE A: ENERGY CENTER
AREAS OF THE BODY

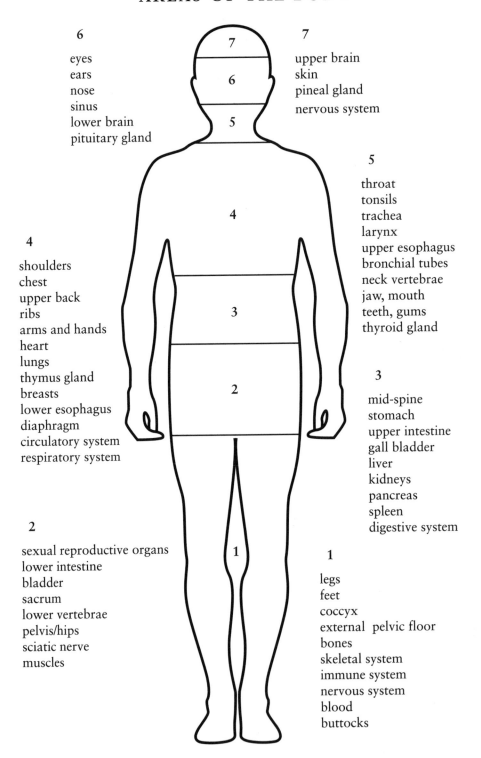

6

eyes
ears
nose
sinus
lower brain
pituitary gland

7

upper brain
skin
pineal gland
nervous system

5

throat
tonsils
trachea
larynx
upper esophagus
bronchial tubes
neck vertebrae
jaw, mouth
teeth, gums
thyroid gland

4

shoulders
chest
upper back
ribs
arms and hands
heart
lungs
thymus gland
breasts
lower esophagus
diaphragm
circulatory system
respiratory system

3

mid-spine
stomach
upper intestine
gall bladder
liver
kidneys
pancreas
spleen
digestive system

2

sexual reproductive organs
lower intestine
bladder
sacrum
lower vertebrae
pelvis/hips
sciatic nerve
muscles

1

legs
feet
coccyx
external pelvic floor
bones
skeletal system
immune system
nervous system
blood
buttocks

THE FIRST ENERGY CENTER

The first center, also appropriately called the root center, governs the feet, legs, external pelvic floor, immune system, bones, blood and buttocks. The belief systems with which this center is linked are directly related to the health of these parts of the body because positive belief systems generally foster a healthy physical body.

The first energy center is programmed to answer questions such as the following:

+ What is the flavor with which I define life? Specifically, where do I fall on the continuum which has "Life is a blessing" at one end and "Life is a burden" at the other?

+ Who has authority over my life?

+ Who made or makes the laws by which I live?

+ Do the laws by which I live limit the energy I bring to my life, or do they liberate energy so that my life is richer?

+ How much influence does my original family (living or dead), or any other group, have over me? (This includes society and the magnetics of mass humanity — in other words, the strong pull to think and behave like everyone else.)

✦ To what degree am I present? (Present means in your body, awake, alert and grounded.)

✦ What is my relationship with the physical world?

✦ How safe and secure do I feel?

✦ Am I supported in my life? Do I feel a sense of stability in my life?

We can see the connection between the areas of the physical body governed by the first energy center, and the belief systems that are energetically stored here. Issues about safety and security relate to our immune systems which provide safety and security for the physical body. Issues of and beliefs about support and stability relate to our skeletal system which provides support and stability for the body. Our original family is called our "blood" relatives, and diseases of the blood can have a link to the way we feel about and relate to our family of origin. The Aquarian Age will bring us insight into ways of reading the body more specifically to determine belief systems that are either supporting or undermining its health.

Besides being the territory for the aforementioned belief systems, the first energy center has another important job. It defines, or flavors, every single experience in our lives. Depending upon the nature of our belief systems, the first center will color our rendition of everything that happens to us. This is like the story of the six blind men describing an elephant. Because each blind man was touching a different part of the animal, each described it in a totally different way. We define what happens to us based on our individualized perspective of how we believe life works. One of the most basic definitions of life is energetically configured in the coccyx, or tailbone, at the very base of the spine. The energetic patterns here place us on the continuum which has "Life is a blessing" at one end and "Life is a burden" at the other. This influences our will to live.

How we define life is basically formed when we are children, especially from conception to about four years old. The belief systems of the people who raise us and have contact with us, the prevailing societal beliefs during that time period, and the influence of other groups, become part of our energetic make-up. At such a young age, we have no ability to make boundaries to refuse these beliefs, which are deposited as energetic configurations in our field.

Every family teaches its children its own brand of physics — the definitions of how life works. All of this comes in through the first energy center. Some beliefs, such as those concerning safety and support, remain energetically configured in the first section of the body; at some point they will affect the physical health of the area of the body governed by the first energy center. The energy of beliefs concerning who is allowed to have power, and how much we personally have, will lodge in the cell tissue of the second section of the body, which deals with these issues. These beliefs will affect the organs and systems associated with that section and energy center. Beliefs about our self-worth will implant in the cell tissue of the third center, and so forth.

In the meantime, all beliefs and experiences will be filed away in an energetic filing system located in the sixth energy center. There our subconscious mind writes the names of our beliefs on the file folders in our particular filing system. Everything we experience is placed in one of the sixth center's file folders. For one person, an experience may be filed under the title "I am a victim," while the same experience will be filed under "I learn about my interior power" for another. Our filing system remains with us for life, unless we do something to change our belief systems, and thus the filing system. (See the section called "The Creative Process" for more specifics.)

The first filing system is set up when we are small children. Therefore, we have no conscious input into it. It is basically installed for us by our family, society and influential groups as we are growing up. This filing system then becomes our blessing or our challenge; usually it is some of both.

The point in our lives when we usually begin to take an in-depth look at the names on our file folders is in our twenties, when the fifth energy center is making a big developmental leap. This is because there is a special relationship between the first center and the fifth center. In our twenties, we are usually moving out into the world to start our own families, our own careers, taking responsibility for ourselves rather than depending on our families to care for us. We are speaking out about what we want, and utilizing the energy of our will to get what we desire. Will, desire, responsibility and speaking out are all energies associated with the fifth energy center. At this point, we physically and/or metaphorically "walk away from" (corresponding to the feet and legs governed by the first energy center) our families, creating a life of our own. We do not usually cut off communication (another fifth center energy) with our families, although we may feel it necessary if our family is strongly trying to prevent us from walking away. This is the point at which we individuate from our families, discerning what inherited belief systems serve us and resonate with us, and which do not, which limit us in life and which bring more energy to our lives. We use the energy of our will (in the fifth center) to do something about those beliefs that we want to transform.

The process of individuation is absolutely essential to the health of the first energy center, and the areas of the body it governs. It is an initiatory stage through which we must pass in order to develop consciously. We claim our authority over our lives, even if we decide to keep many of our family belief systems as our own. We do this as a conscious choice, rather than acting out of fear of the consequences (like the anger of our family or the disdain of society) if we do not follow the inherited "laws."

The planet that is energetically connected with the first energy center is Saturn, which has to do with laws (belief systems), definitions, limitations and authority. In mythology, Saturn's Greek counterpart was Kronos, son of Uranus, god of the heavens, and Gaia, goddess of the earth. Part of Kronos' story rather graphically illustrates the individuation process in a way that is hard to forget. In order to gain his father's throne, Kronos castrated Uranus and put himself in charge of heaven and earth. Symbolically, we look upon this as the child removing the parent's authority over the child's life. The emerging adult then ascends to the throne, to become his or her own "government."

Kronos, also known as Father Time, illustrates another aspect of the first energy center. This center deals with all things of the material world — form, structure and linear time. A function of the first energy center is to connect us kinesthetically with the physical world. Kinesthetic, which has the same etymological base as anaesthetic, comes from Greek words meaning to move and perceive, or movement and sensation. Our first energy center, when healthy, brings us our sensate perception of the world in which we live. It opens specific energetic pathways between our energy fields and that of other people and objects, in order to perceive their physical presence and position. This allows us to clearly define our environment and what is happening in it.

Early trauma before the age of four, especially with regard to safety and stability issues, will damage the development of the first energy center, essentially anaesthetizing it to some degree, and our kinesthetic perception of the world will be distorted. We may have difficulty physically moving through the world, and discerning our presence (physically and emotionally) in relation to other people and objects.

It is our family of origin who can provide us with a sense of safety and security about life. The family can support us in such a way that it contributes to our sense of stability. When this does not happen, we integrate negative beliefs about safety and support into the energy field of our first center. These beliefs show up in our physical stance; if they are retained and acted upon intensely and repeatedly, they can later show up as diseases which affect the immune system, the bones, and the blood. Even when our families deposit positive belief systems regarding safety and support into our energetic makeup, as we become adults, we surely are inundated with the news that there are many unsafe and unsupportive events occurring to people on a regular basis. Looking at our planet and what happens on it every day, we can wonder how we can ever really feel safe and secure.

The gift of feeling safe and supported is attainable through the first center's relationship with the seventh center at the top of the head. Energetically, when this happens, certain energy pathways between the seventh energy center connect with the first center, activating points in the heart area as energy travels between the seventh and the first. The seventh center regulates our sense of and connection with faith and

(margin handwriting: EXPERIENCE CONNECTION WITH DIVINE FORCE)

trust in a compassionate Divine Force. It is only when we viscerally *experience* this connection that we are filled with the knowledge of being held in safety and stability by Spirit. The late Joseph Campbell illustrated this in the story of a young shaman's initiation. Isolated in an igloo for thirty days with only a subsistent supply of water and food, the young man experienced several terrifying hero's journeys. Finally, near the end of his ordeal, he clearly heard a voice which said to him: *Do not be afraid of the universe.* At that point, he was filled with the understanding and sensation of always being held in the safety of Divine Love. Emerging from his initiation, he returned to his tribe to assist them with this concept.

The seventh-first energy centers axis closes the circle of the energy field, allowing a continuous flow from Spirit to matter, from matter to Spirit, from heaven to earth, from earth to heaven. It allows us the internal understanding of the first universal law, the Law of One: Everything comes from the same Source, and that Source is Spirit. The embodiment of this law is another decisive factor in the health of our first energy centers, and thus, the health of our entire lives. It allows us to participate in the synergistic community of life, urges us to create this synergy everywhere, leaving nothing and no one out, but rather encompassing all of creation. When we want to evaluate the energetic health of our first center and the first section of our body, we must evaluate the ways in which we live or do not live the spirit of the Law of One.

The health of every energy center has a direct bearing on the centers adjacent to it, and so the clarity and fullness of our first center directly impacts the health of our second center. The elements which are the dominion of the first energy center lay a foundation on which we build the second energy center. If those elements are missing or faulty, it is like building a house on a faulty foundation. Sooner or later, something will give way. Let us take a look at the second energy center to see how it is impacted by the health of the first.

THE SECOND ENERGY CENTER

Whereas the first energy center defines our experiences, the second center has an emotional response to them. This area of the body, from the internal pelvic floor to the waist, is the energetic region where we have our first emotional response to every single experience we encounter. The emotions involved will always be feelings about ourselves, feelings that grow out of our definition of the experience; both our definition and feeling come from our belief systems. Our families are usually the first to teach us what they consider to be appropriate emotional responses to various experiences, and these responses may range from "Don't have an emotional response" (or at least pretend that you do not, because the emotional response is natural and cannot be stopped), to "Have an explosive emotional response." In the middle of that continuum is an emotional response that comes from a place of balance or equilibrium, which is a quality of a healthy second center.

Because it deals more with emotions than the first center, the physical nature of this area of the body is very different from that of the first area. The second center's body area includes the pelvis and the belly and the lower back. The movement that is possible with this area looks and feels much different from the movement possible with the legs and feet.

The legs and feet feel more structured and supportive; the belly and pelvic girdle can roll and rotate and rock in a sensuous movement, at the same time that it functions as a strong foundation for the upper body. The pelvis is also capable of strong forward and backward thrusts, that suggest a potential power and aggressive force that resides in this part of the body.

Power is a keyword for understanding the second energy center because this center processes the beliefs we have about power: how much we have (which may vary in different situations and with different people), how much everyone else has, what is the proportion of everyone else's power to the amount we have and what "gives" us power. The power arena is the realm of the exuberant Aries Warrior, and its ruling planet Mars, and we can understand this center better by looking at some of the character traits of the mythological god. Mars was filled with energy and vitality. He embodied force and fire. He was a protector and defender as well as a god of fertility. Virile and engaged with life, he desired forward movement and exhibited aggressiveness, courage and passion. He was a god of life-juice and creative expression who inspired and aroused.

The most conscious version of the Mars warrior is one who is a warrior of the heart. Aligned with the compassionate and powerful heart energies, this warrior models power for us by making the hero's journey to fight the interior dragons which represent our biggest fears. Having faced what is feared most, the warrior of the heart transforms fears into active creative power. Consequently, if there are open energetic passageways between the second center and the fourth center (which governs the heart), we have healthy ideas about how to use our power and our warrior energy. When these two centers are disconnected, the warrior moves into the shadow and uses power irresponsibly and detrimentally.

The shadow of Mars is a tendency to be overaggressive and to allow the fiery energy to become uncontained and destructive. When we feel powerless, what do we do to compensate? We may become controlling, we may attack, we may attempt to get even or we may collapse into a victim state. These behaviors emanate from the unhealthy energetic configurations found in the second center. The configurations represent negative beliefs about our lack of power. As we come to be aware of our true internal power during the Aquarian Age, our second energy centers will be reconfigured. A connection between the heart center and the second center will be vital so that we bring the quality of compassion into everything we create with our tremendous inner power.

This warrior of the heart version of evolved Mars energy is aligned with the healthy image of the second energy center — that of the Naked Man or Naked Woman. If we are stripped of all external power and left with nothing but ourselves, can we still be powerful? A healthy second energy center is based on the belief that all our power (and everybody else's) is derived from a Divine Source and is infinite and can never be taken away. This is not a common belief in the world today, where power is synonymous with external trappings. And yet we love the story of the hero who, with everything taken away, is able to find a deep interior well of strength and can use it to manifest the magnificence of the human spirit. To find and access this kind of internal power is one of our challenges in the Aquarian Age.

The positive Mars qualities — vitality, virility, exuberance, passion, forward movement, creative expression, balanced aggression, courage — are energetically encoded in the area of the body governed by the second energy center. If this center is healthy, we find these qualities in our lives. The health of the second center is also built upon the health of the first center. If our first center is depleted or dysfunctional, if we fear for our safety, do not feel supported and suffused by the fire of the will to live, our second energy center cannot possibly be healthy. We do not feel powerful if we never feel safe. We do not feel powerful if we never feel supported. We do not feel the fire of our power if we feel life is too much of a burden, if the fire of our will to live is not strong. Working through issues in the first energy center will naturally affect the second, allowing more flow and communication between the two centers in the lower body.

As always, dysfunction energetically will eventually affect the physical body and compromise the organs and body systems which are governed by the second energy center: the hips, the lower back, the genitals, the reproductive system, the bladder, the lower intestine. The health of these parts of the body partially depends upon the image we hold regarding how powerful we are, what we believe gives us power and what we are willing to do to get it. Any belief that contains an image of a "power ladder" (How many rungs? Which one are we on? Which one is everyone else on?) is illusory and detrimental to our lives.

In mythology, the god Mars married the goddess Venus. Correspondingly there is an intimate connection between the second Mars energy center and the fifth center at the throat which is the domain of the goddess. Because of the marriage between Venus and Mars, we will see aspects of both deities in both the second and the fifth centers.

Both Venus and Mars are associated with desire. The Venus brand of desire is one which urges us to lose ourselves in the pleasure and beauty of the five senses and to balance that with also losing ourselves to the pleasure and beauty of spiritual ecstasy. When Venus is in the second center, in harmonious relationship with Mars, she will manifest as the ability to maintain a sensuous, rolling, rotating physical movement with the pelvis. The belly is soft and open, allowing emotion and sensation to be received. The movement of emotion and sensation through the pelvic area allows a charge to be built up. When it is aligned with the Mars vitality and enthusiasm for moving forward in life, it translates into the power of our sexuality and our creative force.

The Mars desire is a desire to assert oneself on the environment and achieve success in creative endeavors. This entails using aggressive energy to reach out and grasp the creative spark that we are attracted to, and give it direction and impetus to hit the target of its goal. The Mars desire force can be expressed and supported by the exercise of thrusting the pelvis forward, allow it to retract, then thrusting forward again. The strength of the Mars force aligned with the Venus desire force can be strengthened by practicing pelvic rotations. In this exercise, we imagine a pencil on the end of the coccyx, or tailbone, with the point toward the earth. We want to draw big circles with the pencil by isolating a rotating movement in the pelvic area.[22] Both the pelvic thrusts and the pelvic rotations bring energy and high-quality frequencies into the second energy center area of the body.

The health of the second center determines to a large degree the health of the third center above it, in the area of the solar plexus. The third center has to do with self-esteem and how we honor ourselves; it cannot be healthy without a healthy sense of our power and where it really comes from.

THE THIRD ENERGY CENTER

If we feel safe and supported in life, if we take authority for our lives, if we are aware that we have an infinite source of internal power, if we acknowledge, feel and manage our first emotions, we can maintain a healthy third energy center which demands that we honor and pay homage to our being. This center requires that we have respect, admiration, reverence, affection and appreciation for ourselves. It enjoins us to enjoy being the charismatic sovereign of our lives, to value ourselves, be courteous to ourselves, care for ourselves and generally delight in who we are.

The energy of this center corresponds to the energy of the god Jupiter/Zeus, who was king of the gods and resided on the top of the mountain. In the myths, Jupiter/Zeus was quite confident and taken with himself, very sure of his attractiveness and ability to interest and fascinate all who came in contact with him. The Jupiter myths are also filled with stories of excess, which is a shadow energy of the third center. However, Jupiter's very healthy, absolute certainty of his own majesty and splendor, as well as his intention to be his own best friend and staunchest, most loyal ally, made him generous, abundant and jovial. People with healthy third energy centers exude these qualities and fascinate and charm us. They also make us feel comfortable with how comfortable they feel about themselves and who they are; they radiate an expansive energy that is a pleasure to be with.

How we honor ourselves depends upon our beliefs about how good or bad we are. The question "Am I good/good enough?" is the basenote in determining the health of the third energy center. If we believe that we are good, we believe that we deserve good things to come into our life. If we are not so good, then maybe we deserve not so good things, like poisons and toxins. Not coincidentally, one of the organs in the third area of the body is the liver, which processes substances we put into our digestive systems, in order to remove any harmful aspects of those substances.

One of the major jobs of the third center is to maintain our personal space and make sure we are comfortable in it. We can liken this idea of space to an image of a house in which we would like to live. For the house to be comfortable, it should have strong walls, windows and doors which can be opened or closed depending upon what honors us in that moment. Only we should make the decisions about who comes into our house and when, and when that person leaves. In order for this house/personal space to be completely comfortable, we must be discriminatory about who we allow to enter, which is to say, what kind of energy we allow in our house. We must clearly set boundaries to send out the message that intruders, or those who hold energy that does not feel good to us, are not welcome. The third center determines whether we are worthy of having an elegant personal space maintained by clear boundaries; the second center performs the job of enforcing the boundaries to keep our space the way we want it.

Understanding the operation of the digestive system, which is governed by the third energy center, is a wonderful way to understand the psychological dynamics of the third center and the way it must maintain our personal space. Our digestive system performs four main operations,[23] the first of which is to ingest, or take in. If we have healthy eating habits, we only take in foods that are beneficial for us, which will support the soundness and well-being of our physical body at the same time that they bring us pleasure in eating them. If our third energy center is healthy, this positive ingestion will extend into our personal lives. We will not even consider "eating" anything that is toxic to us, or makes us sick or causes us to feel uncomfortable in any way. We use the phrase "I had to eat that" when describing a situation in which we *seem* to have no choice about accepting something unpleasant, or even offensive into our life. Our first job with regard to our third energy center is the same as the first task our digestive system performs, which is to determine that we deserve to have boundaries about what we are willing to accept coming into our bodies, or into our lives. In our house image, if we are faulty with our ingestion process, it is like having doors and windows that cannot close; we are unable to keep out anyone who decides not to honor our personal space. There are those who may attempt to usurp our space, or let us know that they have access to it anytime they want. If we believe that we do not have any power (from the second center), if we believe we are not "good enough" to deserve the right to make a boundary, or if we are afraid of a negative reaction from someone to whom we say "no," we are helpless when this happens.

The amount of consciousness we have concerning the first function of digestion will affect what the second task of the third center/digestive system entails. The second function of the digestive system is to discriminate about whatever has come in and determine if the already ingested substance is good for the body, or if it contains toxins that need to be cleansed by other organs, like the liver and the kidneys. This is when the body separates what is good for us from what is not. It is a second chance to sift out of our bodies/lives what does not honor us.

The ability to discriminate in our lives is of major importance. It concerns our ability to clearly discern a situation which makes us uncomfortable because it does not give us the respect and regard we deserve and our ability to disengage from such situations. The healthy third energy center is able to recognize, identify and label all the things that do not resonate with the reverence, appreciation and loyalty we should have for ourselves, and the subsequent way we care for ourselves. The healthy third energy center then engages the power of the second center to enforce the boundaries it makes; then it sends the toxin to the appropriate place to be cleansed out of our systems.

There are many ways in which society, as well as our original families, may teach us to disregard utilizing the quality of discrimination. We may be taught to accept what feels like poison into our lives with a smile, so that we do not make waves or upset someone. We may not learn that it is okay to say, "This does not feel right to me," because the ramifications may be displeasing to someone else. The challenge of creating a healthy third energy center is to realize that we have the power (from the second center) and the authority (from the first) to draw a line about what we will accept into our lives. Our Jupiter energy should not tolerate anything that feels caustic to us, and that would mean anything that does not contain the energy of self-respect. This is not always easy, especially when the consequences of honoring ourselves make someone else angry, or upset or critical of our behavior. But to accept something that feels bad into our lives is the same as eating poison, and the consequences down the line can be severe.

The third function of the digestive system is that of assimilation. Once we have decided that something is okay, we take in the nutrients it has to offer. If we have ingested toxins, and convinced ourselves that we have no choice but to accept these poisons *as if* they were good food, we feed our bodies/lives with venom rather than nourishment. This is akin to killing ourselves. It knocks our Jupiter right off the mountain, and we become powerless children, relinquishing any authority in our lives to the poisonous situation.

It is possible that we may be able to take in good food, but then not accept its life-giving nutrients. If we have taken high quality food/events/people into our lives, we need to be able to assimilate the benefits they bring. This is connected with the belief that we deserve to be able to connect to the pleasure in life and allow ourselves to revel in joy and good feelings. If we are unable to assimilate, we begin to starve.

The fourth accomplishment that our digestive system carries out for us is that of excretion. This relates to both the third and second energy centers, since the large intestine occupies both areas. Whatever is not useful and beneficial for the body must be eliminated. In our lives, this is akin to throwing out of our house that which we have realized is not good for us, or that we do not need. The root of "excrete" is actually related to the root of "discern," *cernere*, meaning *sift*. We sift out of our lives and let go of what does not honor us, what does not pay homage to the glory and splendor that is our essence.

The third energy center is also the center from which we radiate out energy in order to connect with people. Healthy Jupiter energy is friendly and outgoing. It flows out, seeking to expand our affiliations. When we are exploring the idea of connecting with someone we send out a streamer of energy from this center to meet with the field of the other person and investigate what his or her energy feels like. With this streamer of energy we read, either consciously or unconsciously, the other person energetically. As this information comes back to us, we sift through it and make choices about how to proceed. When the third center is not healthy, we are not able to consciously register any uncomfortable sensations that come back to us from this exploratory energy streamer. Or we may only register the ways in which the other person's energy is manipulatively stroking our Jupiter energy; this makes us feel majestic from the outside, when actually we question our internal majesty. In these cases, the choices we make about how to proceed into relationship (which will be handled by the fourth energy center) will have the potential to bring even more discomfort into our lives.

We also establish caretaking cords with other people from the third energy center.[24] These streamers of energy connect us with people who need our care in some way. This would happen between a parent and a child, as the parent must provide care for the child that the child is not capable of providing for itself. The caretaking connections between parents and children should naturally begin to dissolve as the child grows older and becomes more self-sufficient. If this does not happen, and the parent is putting too much caretaking energy into the child when it is not necessary, the child can rebel and rip the cord, which is painful. This happens commonly in adolescence, as parents and children must adapt to new relationship dynamics. Or the child can leave the cord, and grow up with little sense of his or her own responsibility. At this point the caretaking cord becomes a burden on the parent, as s/he must not only take responsibility for him/herself, but also for someone else. This is like carrying someone else's baggage as well as our own. If we tend to do this for too many people, we will soon become overwhelmed by our burden.

The field around our third energy center can get damaged by someone who attacks our sense of who we are. If we are unsure about how "good" we are, or if we deserve honor, a single remark that questions these beliefs can cause substantial damage to the energy field in this part of the body. When the field is damaged in such a way, we feel terrible about ourselves. Depending upon the degree to which this happens, we can become unable to function. A mother once brought her twelve-year-old daughter to my office for healing work because the child was depressed, refused to go to school and was throwing up every morning. The field around her third energy center was distorted. When this was repaired, the child was able to talk about a situation that had occurred in school, in which several friends verbally attacked her, adversely affecting her vulnerable self-image and damaging the field. After the energy work, she was able to return to school and deal with her peers who had hurt her.

The third center also processes our opinions about every experience that occurs. Remember that the first energy center defines the experience and the second produces an emotion regarding it. Now the third produces thoughtforms and opinions about what has happened. These thoughts naturally are aligned with our definition and feelings. Because of its role in processing opinions, the third center is sometimes called a "mental" center.

In order to create a healthy image for our third energy centers, we can imagine some of the great rulers from history and the present. A person who is considered a magnificent leader, exhibits the qualities of the third center — firmness and dominance *balanced with* the ability to yield when necessary, patience and compliance poised with authority.

The highest vibration we can bring to our third energy centers is to associate our sovereignty, our most powerful potentate, with our Higher Self. The Higher Self is that part of us that is constantly aware of our connection to a Greater Force, called Spirit, or God. Our Higher Self guides us constantly, is compassionately and passionately fond of us and treasures us even when we make mistakes. A strong connection with the seventh energy center can bring this healing vibration to the third center. An open passageway with the fourth center of the heart is also necessary so that compassion and love can filter into our esteem for ourselves, and ensure that the way we treat ourselves is honorable.

THE FOURTH ENERGY CENTER

The fourth energy center is the heart center. It governs the region of the physical body from the diaphragm to the base of the throat, regulating all the organs in this part of the body, as well as the circulatory system.

The fourth center has a magical quality to it because of its ability to transform lower vibrational energies into higher ones. In fact, one of the functions of the fourth center is to process the first emotion generated in the second center and transform that emotion, if necessary. Any emotion, like anger, which would prompt a negative response from us (response occurs in the next center, the fifth) has the opportunity to be transformed (which is actually to have its vibration raised), as the energy of the emotion passes through the fourth center. When we add heart energy to any emotion, that emotion is lifted up to become the "best" that it can be.

This alchemical ability of the heart center is directly linked to the energy that radiates from the center — the energy of love, which in turn engenders compassion and forgiveness. The clarity of the heart center, and the proficiency with which it is able to do its transformative job, depends upon our ability to feel, give and receive love. This includes the idea of feeling love for ourselves, as well as for all of life. The open heart allows us to be compassionate towards all of life, allowing powerful energetic radiations to stream out from our fourth energy center and bless everything they touch. The open heart center allows us to forgive (not condone) the negative actions of others as well as ourselves. When we forgive, we do not stay negatively chained to someone who has "done us wrong." The quality of forgiving allows us to move forward in our lives.

We truly experience the magic of the fourth center when we are "in love." This is a miraculous time when we are less defensive and much more willing to be compassionate toward others, including ourselves. We glow when we are in love; we visibly radiate love's energy. Our lives feel different and reconstructed in positive ways. Our hearts are open and the energy of love bathes every experience, raising the vibration of the experience so that we are more able to discern the beauty of Spirit all around us in our physical world. Everything is brighter, clearer, more exciting, more delicious. Life takes on a radiance that is limited by our attempts to describe it in language.

Are we aware that we carry the treasure of this energy with us, at our disposal at all times? Are we aware that we always have the capability to imbue our life with joy, peace, harmony and balance? It would seem that a disciplined practice of learning to upwell the heart energy would certainly be, not only in our best interest, but in the best interest of the entire planet. This practice can be started by simply focusing on someone or something that we love. If we cannot find something to love, we need to look for something because having something to love is a jumping-off point to more powerfully wonderful heart states of being. This kind of "heart practice," a mandate of the Piscean Age which we are now leaving, becomes an absolutely necessary foundation for moving into the new age of Aquarius.

The heart center is also called the bridge between the lower energy centers and the three centers above it. The lower centers, sometimes referred to as the world of matter, guide us with regard to how we maneuver in the physical plane. The upper three centers represent the world of Spirit and remind us to incorporate a sense of the Divine in the earthly dimension. We cannot get from the world of matter to the world of spirit without passing through the heart center. It is the energy of the heart center that allows us to infuse our daily life in the world of matter with the Light of the One Force.

In keeping with this, the astrological "planet" associated with the heart center is the sun. Mythologically and as a historical symbol, the sun represents a supreme god or force, unlimited possibility and infinite life energy. It is the essence of consciousness, the juice of life, the illuminator that brings us visceral awareness of the Divine breath that is the basis of our lives. The energy of the sun bestows life to the universe, brings harmony, dispels darkness and allows us to recognize life's inherent beauty.

Like the physical sun, the healthy fourth center radiates a warm energy that has life-giving properties. As the energy of the fourth center shines on any other center, it brings to life the qualities of that center, making the center, and subsequently our lives, healthy and whole. When its energy is paired with the three lower centers, we are able to maneuver through life with ease and harmony, maintaining a balance between the earthly dimension that is our present home and the spiritual dimension from which we are born.

An energetic yoke between the first and fourth centers bring stability and safety into our lives and allows us to be spontaneous. This alliance allows us to be aware of our relationship with the earth and sense the living spiritual energy of the planet. The heart center allows us to feel Saturn's solitude as peace, rather than loneliness. As we take authority for what kind of life we will live, the heart's qualities empower us to incorporate Spirit into that life.

When the rays of the sun center shine on the pelvic area of the body, governed by the Mars warrior energy, it infuses the warrior with all the gifts of the heart. The heart aligns the positive forward movement of the second energy center with the energy of compassion. The association between the heart and second centers creates the courageous hero who faces and conquers his or her interior dragons to lift the consciousness of the whole world.

The heart center has a major influence on the adjacent third energy center of the body. To be the charismatic sovereign of our lives, our Jupiter must have a healthy sense of self-love. The fourth center energies of devotion, affection, fondness, commitment, warmth and appreciation need to flow into the third center to be bestowed upon ourselves. If these qualities are missing, our Jupiter can easily become an insecure tyrant, and we are unable to manifest the heart center energies toward anyone else because we believe we cannot have them for ourselves.

An interesting imbalance between the fourth and third centers can commonly occur. The third center denotes our ability to make comfortable boundaries for ourselves; the fourth gives us the capacity to radiate love. These two aptitudes should be complementary, but it is common to be taught, by society and/or our original family, that they can exist only in opposition to each other. This results in the perception that if we give out love to others, we cannot maintain a comfortable boundary for ourselves; disseminating love is at the expense of what feels okay for us. Conversely, if we endorse a boundary because it honors us, we cannot radiate love and compassion. The belief that maintaining healthy boundaries and giving out love are exclusive of each other creates an energy block, which manifest as two repellent magnetic force fields (one representing the magnetics of the fourth energy center, the other representing the magnetics of the third center) in the diaphragm, the large sheet of muscle that separates the chest and abdominal cavity. Because the force fields repel each other, the energy flow between the two centers is difficult and impeded. The result is that if the heart center opens, the third center closes; if the third center opens, the fourth center closes down. This distortion is caused by a perception that severely limits our definition of love and burdens our right to provide ourselves with boundaries that allow us to feel at ease.

The majority of the parts of the body and the organs which are governed by the fourth energy center are paired. In this region of the body we have two arms, hands, wrists, elbows, shoulders, collar bones, lungs, breasts, rib cages, as well as a double-lobed thymus gland. The heart is in a double sac, and looks like two chambers combined as one organ. The pairing of organs and parts of the body is a symbol of a major function of this energetic center, which is to process the way in which we establish and maintain relationships with others. The energy from this center encompasses both masculine and feminine vibrations. The magnetic attraction between these two polarities, riding on the waves of the frequency of love, results in an internal marriage that brings balance, harmony and beauty into our lives.

Our beliefs about relationships contribute to creating the health of the energy field in this part of the body; subsequently our perceptions regarding relationships also affect the physical body. Our ability to allow the emotions engendered by relationships to flow and move and be felt by us, is directly related to how effectively the physical heart operates. The heart itself, with its two chambers combined as one organ, physically represents a synergistic union which results in an incredibly powerful creation, one which is representative of the infinite power of the sun, of the One Force which creates and sustains the universe. Through the circulatory system, also under the dominion of the fourth energy center, this Force is dispersed throughout the body, throughout our lives, throughout our world.

We begin to really feel the activation of the heart center during adolescence. We become more acutely aware of the heart qualities of adventure and freedom, as well as feeling the force of emotions generated by our relationships with others. All of this at once can be quite a turbulent mix, and the developmental period of adolescence illustrates this. We experiment with many of our views about how life works during this time. Specifically, we explore beliefs about how to love, how lovable we are, how safe it is to feel emotions, what relationships are about, how we will handle freedom or the lack of it and whether or not our warriors (the Mars energy in the second center) will become aligned with our heart energy. Because it is rare for adolescents to have a wise adult well-versed in heart energy to guide them with the development of this all-important center, what emerges during this time may be out-of-sync with the gifts of peace, balance and beauty that a stable healthy heart center bestows. However, no matter how old we are, it is never too late to retrieve these gifts through a process of self-examination and intentional awareness.

THE FIFTH ENERGY CENTER

This area of the body, from the base of the throat to just under the ears and nose, energetically processes the relationship we establish between two powerful forces — desire and the will.

The energies of desire and the will share the space of the fifth center, with desire residing in the softer front area and the will making its headquarters in the back, in the cervical vertebrae of the spine. This makes sense since we think of will as strong, resolute and determined; the dense hard bone tissue is the perfect place to house such an energy. Desire, on the other hand, has to do with longing and yearning, a hunger that makes our jaws drop, our saliva flow and can bring a smile to our face; hence, desire resides in the front aspect of the throat center.

The energy of our will is available to carry out our desire. When our desire creates a target or goal, and we aim the arrow of our attention at it, it is our will that gives the arrow the driving thrust forward, the impetus that carries it through the air to hit the bulls-eye. We all have the same, infinite amount of will power, because our will is simply an aspect of Divine Will, which is all the will power in the universe. It is our belief systems that limit our idea of how much will power we have.

Likewise, we hold beliefs regarding our desires, which can be explored by answering questions like: Is it okay to have desires? How difficult are they to fulfill? When we have open roadways between our heart center and our throat center, our desires and our will are linked with the energy of love and compassion. When this happens, the fulfilling of our desires will, on some level, benefit the entire planet. When there is no dialogue between these two centers, our will and desire are bereft of the heart energies and have the potential to do more harm than good.

The goddess Venus, linked with the throat center, is the goddess of beauty and desire, and her goal is to urge humanity to lose itself in the ecstasy of both sensual and spiritual pleasure. The goddess of creative imagination, Venus wants to create beauty everywhere. Her energy is lush and rich and fertile and she is always ready to birth something new. This creative force resides in the energetic throat area, always available to burst forth new possibilities into our lives.

Since Venus ended up marrying the god Mars, we find him in the throat center as well. In the fifth center, we can equate Mars with the will energy, the masculine energy which initiates the creative process, reaching for and grasping the Divine spark which is then received by Venus. Venus incubates what she receives from Mars, multiplies it, shapes it and gives birth to it. This is the Law of Gender in operation.

Because the fifth center houses the throat and the voice, it also processes our communication skills and the beliefs we have about being able to communicate, speak out and speak truthfully. Communication implies interaction with someone else, so once again, an open relationship with the heart center solidifies our ability to connect with and touch people by what we say or write. When the heart center energies flow through the fifth center, they spur the emergence of truth, honesty and authenticity from the energetic throat area.

By listening to the timbre of our voice, we can gauge how the energy in our throat is flowing. It can move along a continuum from gushing to restrained. This continuum is also in play as the energetic throat center processes our experiences by responding to them with expressions that range from expansive loving kindness to contracted and severe constraint. If our will is a tyrannical Mars, squelching the Venus energy in addition to denying the existence of the heart, we will react, rather than respond, to our experiences with a show of severity, criticism and judgment, with the possibility of an explosive release of negative emotions. If Venus is demanding, greedy and disconnected from heart energy, we will have too much permissiveness in our lives, giving in to every unexamined desire.

Although the energy of the will is based in the back of the throat center, its territory includes the entire spinal column, where it continuously travels and reveals itself in relationship to the second, third, fourth and sixth centers in their back aspects, and also in relationship to the first center which governs the coccyx, the last vertebrae at the base of the spine. The tissue in the coccyx holds the energetic configurations representing the belief system continuum with regard to the will to live (an aspect of will power) which states: "Life is a blessing" or "Life is a burden," and the entire range in between. It is our family of origin who basically gives to us the belief system regarding life's boons versus life's afflictions. This affects the way we accept the energy of what we experience and the way we take it into our bodies and our lives. The coccyx is energetically programmed to either receive the energy gracefully (Life is a blessing) or with resistance (Life is a burden). Based on the belief system in the cell tissue of the coccyx, the energy of everything we experience is then programmed as to how, and if, it will move up the spine.

If the will-to-live belief systems are healthy, energy coming into the first center and the coccyx is distributed into the proper flow patterns. Then the sacrum, in the back aspect of the second energy center, takes the energy with the statement: "I have enough power to carry this sacred life; I can be a foundation for it." The will energy then flows through the back of the second easily on its way up the spine. When energy flows like this, we feel creatively and sexually powerful. We are aware of our power to govern and regulate our environment. When the energy in the back of the second center is out of control and not in balance with the front, we will use our will power in attempts to control what is not within our right to control. Will power will be used to manipulate and take control over others.

When we fear that we cannot carry what life brings us, the energy in the back of the second will be blocked or distorted in some way. We sometimes use held or suppressed emotions (remember, the second center generates our first emotional response or reaction to our experiences) as substitute "foundational stones" in order to create passageways to carry the will energy. These may even work in the short run, but the falsely fabricated structure will eventually collapse and leave us in crisis.

The will energy passing through the third center allows us to carry out actions that will honor us, including taking action to be comfortable, as well as our ability to physically care for ourselves. The will energy in the back of the third center supports our Jupiter, our charismatic sovereignty over our life. When energy is not passing through this center in the proper flow patterns, with the proper vibrational rate, it will manifest itself as some degree of inability to take care of ourselves well — from basic necessities to self care when we are sick. Distorted energy here also manifests as the inability to say no and know that we have the right to make healthy boundaries when someone intrudes upon us.

Will energy flowing healthily through the back of the heart center manifests itself as an appropriate sense of what place the will has in our relationships, and the balance between love and will that we maintain in our interactions. Healer and author Barbara Ann Brennan states that the energy running through the back aspect of the heart center has to do with how we view the role that other people play when we want to accomplish something.[25] Will other people support us, or will they make it more difficult for us to get what we want? If the latter is true, we certainly believe we cannot be loving and compassionate, so we pull energy out of the front aspect of the fourth center and into the back. The heart is then not involved in our relationships; to some degree, we decrease our compassion for humanity, for life. When this pattern is strong and habitual, it can produce a potentially frightening type of person — one who can have great will power while at the same time defining the term "cold-hearted" at its extreme.

The will energy that resides in the back of the fifth, or throat, center, also has to do with what is happening in our lives when this center is finishing its full development. This time of our life is post-adolescence, in our twenties, when we are traditionally moving out into the world on our own, starting a career, creating our own families, individuating from our original family. If the energy in the back of the fifth center is healthy, we are able to use our will to accomplish all these things. If the energy is deficient in any way, we will create obstacles with regard to these goals.

THE SIXTH ENERGY CENTER

We use our will energy to act upon all the belief systems we hold. The filing system for our beliefs is held in the sixth energy center. Belief systems that are inherited, as well as those that we create, are energetically filed in the sixth energy center. There they are called upon as we experience life; when we have an experience, a certain file is opened in the sixth center and we respond in a patterned manner to the experience.

For example, we may have labeled an incident that happened to us when we were a child as "I can be hurt." This becomes a name on a file folder. Henceforth, any incidents that resonate with the original wounding experience, any incidents that contain a similar vibrational rate, will cause our sixth center to pull out the file labeled "I can be hurt." In this file is recorded a formula for defining any events that have harmonic resonances with the original wounding experience. The formula generates, into our present-day life, emotions and thoughtforms associated with the childhood "I can be hurt" incident. The pulling of this file begins to set in motion a computer program that puts specific energetic configurations (representing our definition, and the accompanying thoughts and feelings) into the energy field. These configurations arrange the field in a defensive and distorted posture. Since the field is our personality, we now behave in defensive and distorted ways, trying to protect ourselves as we did when we were children. For all intents and purposes, we are flashed back to the original wound that we experienced and are caught in a time warp that dictates our behavior.

The pulling of the file marked "I can be hurt" automatically opens a series of sub-files which specifically affect the energy patterns of each energy center. So, a sub-file named "I am not safe" awakens distorted energetic programming in the first energy center, which deals with issues of safety. A sub-file for the second center might be "I am powerless"; the sub-file for the third center might be called "I must be bad," and so forth. All these sub-files contain the habitual definitions, thoughts and painful emotions that accompany the stated belief name on the file.

As the sub-files are put into play, each energy center is impeded. We feel terrible and can whirlpool down into a black hole. We might use up most of our energy in an attempt to suppress the painful emotions; consequently, we wind up depressed. Both the energy of suppressed emotions as well as habitual negative emotions running through our field will eventually have an impact on the denser levels of our physicality and disease will manifest.

In a line above the top of the eyebrows, and at certain places on the forehead, there are energetic points which are emotional-receptor sites. Using these points, it is possible to short circuit a negative computer program from being played. These sites activate the emotional configurations associated with any belief system. When the belief is negative and the corresponding emotions are painful, we can put clear energy into these sites and it can short-circuit the emotional part of the negative computer program. If the distressing emotions are never put into play, or only run for a very short time, it is much easier to abort the entire negative program.

We do this short-circuiting quite naturally. When we are upset or dealing with painful emotions, we many times hold our forehead in our hand, covering the receptor sites. We stroke the brow of a child, or someone in emotional pain, with a loving, compassionate touch. We can also place our fingers across someone's brow, as if we were preparing to play the piano, and allow loving energy to flow through our fingers into the receptor sites. These actions stymie the process of flooding the field with negative emotions.

Sometimes it takes a resonance that is only a hint of the original offending energy to pull a certain file and spark the subsequent distorted behavior and thought patterns. The healing of our wounds finally takes place when we are able to put new names on our negative file folders. This means we have gained *insight* about the our original wounding experience which allows us to detach from our negative, illusory beliefs. This is the work of self-awareness and evolving consciousness, and it always involves the transformative heart energies. Now, even though a present-day incident resonates with an original wound, we *perceive* the incident differently. The relabeled file folder contains a program to spark energetic configurations that arrange our field in an entirely different way than before. Rather than shutting down and distorting, we open up and allow more Divine Force to flow through us, activating the wholeness of each energy center. Different thoughtforms and different emotions automatically accompany the insightful statement on the newly labeled folder.

The sixth energy center is also the doorway to the subconscious mind. (See the section called "The Creative Process" for more information about the way the subconscious mind works.) Subconsciousness never changes the name on a file folder. Only our waking consciousness can do that. However, the powerful subconsciousness, which is in touch with all points in space, does connect us with people and experiences which support our belief systems, whether they be positive or negative. So if we open the "I can be hurt" file, not only will we experience the painful feelings and thoughts that go along with that belief, but our subconsciousness will begin to network for us, finding people and setting up experiences that will continue to make us feel that we can be hurt. The names on the file folders instruct our subconsciousness to give our field a certain magnetic charge that will attract to us exactly what we believe. This is the creative process, and when we neglect to go through our belief filing system and change negative file names to positive ones, we are passively accepting whatever life brings us, based on how we interpreted life *as a child*. The majority of our experiences will then be calibrated to whatever childhood self gave the name to the file folder.

The sixth center also houses both our intuition and our rational, linear mind. As mentioned previously, these two assets share the office space of the sixth center. In balance, the two support and feed each other, bringing us the qualities of wisdom and empathetic understanding. When this happens, our ideas are not only based in sound rationality, but also laced with insight and its intuitional sense of perceptive understanding.

Supervised by the moon, the sixth center supplies us with our sense of the rhythm and periodicity of life. Astrologer Caroline Casey states that the moon governs the inner tides of our feelings and moods. This makes perfect sense, considering that the energetic emotional receptor sites are located in this part of the body. When our sixth center is not functioning well, the rhythm of our emotions and attitudes are one-sided, lacking or too intense.

The moon is connected with the consciousness of mass humanity. This is humanity's average level of self-awareness, and unfortunately, at this time it is not a very positive vibration. Listening to the news, we can be aware that most people's lives deviate from following Divine Law and there is a tremendous deficit of ability to feel loved and give out love. Our sixth energy center can detect the energy of mass consciousness as its tide flows into us from the universal energy field that encompasses our planet. One of the challenges we are faced with is not to be influenced by the very strong magnetics of mass consciousness. If we are, our filing system is affected, and subsequently, so is our behavior. If our sixth center is awake, we can recognize and clearly name low vibrational behavior, thoughtforms and emotions that are connected with the negative belief systems of mass consciousness. Then we have a choice as to whether to let the tide take us, or to forge a path of our own.

The sixth center houses our inspiration, which sparks our imagination. The ability to consciously imagine is an absolutely necessary step in the creative process. If we cannot imagine something, we cannot create it. Healthy use of the sixth center includes seeking out what inspires us so that we can set in motion the wheels of positive conscious imaging. Of course, negative imaging will also bring forth results, so it is very necessary to monitor what our imagination is producing.

If the front and back aspects of the sixth center are working with each other, the ideas and images that are created in the front aspect flow through to the back aspect, which has to do with carrying out our ideas and making them manifest in our lives. When the two are in disharmony, we may have great ideas, but no ability to see them through to creation.

THE SEVENTH ENERGY CENTER

The seventh energy center monitors our transition into other dimensions, such as those of altered states, sleep, coma, death and the Light realm of Divine Force. It functions as an energetic roadway that facilitates our movement into territory other than the earthly dimension. It is the center through which our energy is released from the physical body when we die. It can also be a passageway that we use to evacuate our energy from the body when we get scared, or experience trauma. When we do this, we are essentially running away from the physical plane because it frightens us. We run into the arms of a Divine Force, knowing that there we will experience safety and support and unconditional love.

The seventh center is our link with Spirit, and we activate and strengthen it every time we pray. It contains the energetic configuration of the quality of faith and also holds all our beliefs about a Higher Power. It can be a channel for receiving the gifts of Spirit, which bring us everything that we need, in any area of our life.

The energy of Mercury presides over the seventh center. In mythology, it was the job of the messenger god Mercury to be the mediator between the gods and humanity. Mercury brought the wisdom of the higher spiritual realms to the earth, and by doing so encouraged the transformational process. In esoteric Tarot, Mercury is represented by Key 1, the Magician, who stands with his right hand raised to the heavens and his left hand pointing downward. This stance indicates the job of the Magician — to reach for Divine Force and channel Its power into the earthly dimension. Once again, this represents the creative process.

The Magician's talent lies in being able to focus his or her attention on what he wants. Likewise, the seventh center bestows upon us the quality of attention, the ability to concentrate energy on a goal in order to bring it to life. The act of paying attention to something aligns our sixth center and seventh energy centers and allows them to connect with the will energy in the fifth. The impetus of the will provides the force to send the focused energy exactly where we want it to go.

In this way, the seventh center can be said to be the home of our waking conscious minds. The waking consciousness, like the messenger god, mediates between what we call superconsciousness (that part of us that is linked to Divine Forces, sometimes called the Higher Self) and subconsciousness in the sixth center. When waking consciousness can be a clear channel, the Divine energies of Spirit can travel directly and cleanly through to direct the subconscious to connect us with what we want to create. Then whatever we create will be linked with Spirit, and will have the ability to bring more Spirit into our life and the lives of all humanity.

Another quality associated with the seventh energy center is that of surrender or release. Think of the word "surrender" as being linked with the idea of acquiescence and consent, as giving permission and accepting, rather than with the idea of submitting to someone else's control. The idea of release can likewise be defined as freedom and liberation that delivers independence. In order to be connected with Spirit, we must surrender to its Force, accepting It as the guiding and loving Authority in our lives. We acquiesce to the idea that our personalities are not the main show; they are merely structures that are perfectly suited to carry the Force of Spirit into our lives. Upon this acceptance, we experience a sensation of release, of freedom from fear, emancipation from negative beliefs, and utter independence as we reclaim our birthright of our true selves.

The idea of release also applies to the final step on the journey an experience makes through our energy system. If we have allowed any negative emotions to be transformed by the heart center, which will then alter and modulate our response to the experience in the fifth center, if we have gained the insight from the experience in the sixth center, then we are ready to release it in the seventh. We have gleaned the gold (a color of the seventh center) from the experience; we retain what we have learned from the experience, and no longer need to carry the energy of it in our system.

Whenever we have "unfinished business" with anyone in our lives, we have yet to release the experience from our fields through the seventh center. The negativity of the experience continues to circulate through our field, poisoning our lives and our bodies. Learning from all our experiences, and letting them go, is a challenge of evolving consciousness.

The seventh center has a direct line to the sacred gold of our Higher Self, that part of who we are that is continuously aware of our connection with and birth from a Divine Source. Our Higher Self will guide us constantly and accurately, if we allow it. Like the Hermit in the picture on Tarot Key 9, our Higher Self holds the lantern for us as we negotiate the journey up the mountain. It keeps our task, the reason we are on the earth, in our consciousness, and reminds us of the totality of who we truly are.

SYMBOLIC INTERPRETATION:

FINDING SPIRITUAL DIRECTIVES IN EVERYDAY LIFE

AN OUTLINE FOR SYMBOLIC READING	

First Level: Literal	1. Write a page-long description of the situation to be assessed.
	  a. Name facts.
	  b. Describe any feelings you have.
	2. Re-read what is written. Circle:
	  a. Charged words and phrases
	  b. Repeated words and phrases
	  c. Body vocabulary

Second Level: Symbolic/ Metaphorical	1. Use circled words to create new sentences, poems or stories.
	2. Employ writing practice. Use as a theme:
	  a. The situation to be assessed
	  b. Any circled words or phrases
	3. Listen to your body.
	  a. Notice physiological responses to the situation.
	  b. Translate what happens and write it down.
	4. Ask the right questions.
	  a. What does the situation prevent me from doing?
	  b. What does the situation force me to do?
	5. Check for dissonance with universal law.
	6. Find a central theme.
	  a. Look for repetitious statements.
	  b. Use a dictionary of symbols to decode images.
	  c. Make metaphors from the circled words and phrases.

Third Level: Irrational/ Non-logical	1. Practice quieting the linear mind.
	  a. Employ writing practice at least 30 minutes a day.
	  b. Meditate and immediately write in your journal afterwards.
	  c. Search for distorted beliefs through the practice of meditation.
	2. Re-explore the metaphors unearthed in the second level.
	  a. Feel their discordance in your body.
	  b. Match this discordance with your life.
	  c. Pray to become more clear in this regard.
	3. Allow yourself to experience how bad it feels to be in dissonance with universal law.

Fourth Level: Meaning/ Mystery	1. Pray, meditate, ask and reach for the mystery.
	2. Surrender to the not-knowing state.
	3. Open to the direction of the Will-to-Good.
	4. Make a habit of 1, 2 and 3.
	5. Notice negative beliefs that keep you separate from God.
	  a. Align your intention not to participate in them.
	  b. Instruct your will not to energize them.
	  c. Take the risk that they are illusory.
	6. Turn the situation over to the Greater Force.
	7. Open the heart.
	8. Pray even more.

A FRAMEWORK FOR
SYMBOLIC READING

An attribute of Spirit is that it always contains messages for us which will provoke insights that lead us into higher consciousness. We can learn to unveil and translate guidance and direction from Spirit in any thing, any one and any event. The art of symbolic interpretation is the ability to extract wisdom and clarity from whatever touches our lives, the ability to interpret human events and find the spiritual directives encoded therein. When the spiritual directive is followed, the baser energies of the event are transformed into Divine energies. In this way, healing takes place.

Symbolic interpretation is actually the job that our spiritual leaders now hold — the capacity to take in an experience and evaluate it at levels much deeper than the superficial way that we are used to looking at things. The deeper evaluation allows us to understand the intrinsic spiritual directive in the experience. It is the job of our spiritual leaders to then give the experience back to us in a way that expands our understanding of it in accordance with the Divine Plan and at the same time brings us some solace.

In the Age of Aquarius, we will be asked to learn to do this for ourselves. How can we begin to become masters of unearthing the messages Spirit sends us? Four basic steps are helpful to interpret and translate the spiritual missives encoded within every experience.

In a 1994 seminar entitled "The Language of the Body/Mind: A Body Symbology Workshop," healer and author Reverend Rosalyn Bruyere set forth four steps for interpreting the spiritual messages brought to us via our disease. In an audiotape called *The Mystical Kabbalah*, Rabbi David Cooper names four steps to use to interpret sacred teachings. The steps for interpreting sacred teachings and the steps for interpreting disease are exactly the same. This is because both focus on reading symbolically, which is the same as reading energetically, which is the same as uncovering spiritual messages in the physical plane.

Bruyere's/Cooper's steps provide a structure into which we can plug an event, a physical condition, a person's behavior, a world crisis or the words of the mystics. The four levels of interpretation are the literal level, the symbolic/metaphorical level, the irrational/non-logical level and the meaning/mystery level.

Moving through these levels allows us to embark on a journey of using what is happening in our lives as an impetus for growth of consciousness. Our intention when we start out can be stated as: "I have chaos/discomfort/pain/disease/trauma in my life and I would like to make sense of it. I would like to make the best I can of this situation. I am willing to allow for the possibility that I can come to terms with what is occurring, and also evolve my consciousness, no matter what changes that brings into my life."

This is different from merely asking "Why is this always happening to me?" Although this question may be our first, and very human, reaction to our chaos, trying to get an answer to why we were singled out for a particular experience is like questioning whether Spirit really knows what It is doing. Especially when the chaos we are experiencing is terribly painful and seemingly irrational, there is no answer to the question "Why?" that will bring us any degree of comfort. An *explanation* of tragedy is impossible. It takes faith, courage and surrender to a Force which is greater than we are to move through our pain to an expanded *awareness* of what role tragedy plays in our lives.

The place of healing is a place of coming to terms with our pain. It is essentially the transformation of lower energies to higher ones, as we allow the Light of Spirit to come into our energy fields. Journeying through the four levels of interpretation allows this transformation and brings us to the expanded place where we can heal and experience peace, clarity and the gift inherent in all of life, *even if the chaos itself does not change.*

The movement through the four levels will raise our consciousness. This means that our lives will change in some way, from shifts in the way we think, to changes in our behavior, to decisions to make major alterations of our life circumstances. We cannot move through the four levels without change occurring. We must accept this fact or we will unconsciously block our own path to prevent change from happening. When setting out, we may not have a clear idea of how change will need to manifest itself in our lives. That is to be expected; it is the reason we need to make the journey in the first place. But it is important to know that, unconsciously, we may first dig in our heels at the prospect that we are deliberately setting out to upset our status quo.

THE LITERAL LEVEL

What You See Is What You Get

We begin with the literal level, the level where we most often completely base our experience. This is the "what you see is what you get" level. Things are what they are and there is no hidden meaning anywhere. The literal level is important because it is a ground from which to start. It is a place where we interpret what is happening through our five senses. On the literal level, we use our linear minds and our intellectual faculties to name, define and describe the situation we want to assess; however this is done through the veil of our present consciousness which includes all our belief systems, positive and negative. On this level we hold the "baser energies" which the god Mercury sought to transform by bringing in Divine wisdom.

In order to define the starting point of our "base" energies, we write an at-least page-long description of the situation we wish to assess, stating the facts (as we see them) and naming and describing any feelings we are having. This first writing exercise is the beginning of a journal we will keep as we move through the four levels. Once this description is finished, we re-read what is written and circle the "charged" words, the words that stand out for us, words and phrases that feel strong or carry the meat of the description. We also notice and circle any words or phrases that are repeated, and any phrases that contain the names of parts of the body, such as "This situation is a real pain in the neck," or "It is tearing my heart apart."

Once the description is to our liking, we are ready to begin working with the second level of interpretation.

THE SYMBOLIC/
METAPHORICAL LEVEL

On this level, we first explore the vocabulary we used to write our first-level description. We engage in word play to unearth subconscious images and we learn the art of something called writing practice. We pay attention to our physiological responses to the situation that we are assessing. We evaluate it according to its resonance or dissonance with universal law. We ask ourselves specific questions which, with the information we have gathered so far, assist us to come up with a central theme around which our situation revolves.

Let's take a look at each of these steps in detail.

Exploring Our Vocabulary

The exploration of the vocabulary we used to describe the event or situation we wish to assess is a bridge from the literal to the symbolic level. When we are trying to read a situation energetically, it is usually because the situation is troublesome in some way, which means it is a warning signal that there is an area of our lives that needs to be transformed. The vocabulary we use on the literal level gives us clues about the direction in which we should be looking to find that place in need of transformation. Our terminology is connected to the belief systems that are playing a foundational role in supporting what is uncomfortable or painful in our life. If we take the circled words from our literal description, we can link them together in sentences which describe the ways in which we believe life works, and therefore, the ways in which our subconsciousness hears that we *want* life to work, and structures our life accordingly. On the symbolic level, we make the quantum leap to acknowledging that the words we use send energetic messages to our body (especially if body parts are named) and our subconscious mind, and everything is interpreted *literally*. Subconsciousness then directs our body to perform in exactly the way it has been told. (See the section called "The Creative Process" for more specifics about how this works.)

The exercise of linking the circled words is a good one; it is like that old elementary school homework exercise of "Write a paragraph using these vocabulary words." We can play with the circled words and phrases and see what comes up: a poem, a story or just some sentences. We can write each word or phrase on an index card and put all the cards on our desk. Each day, we move them around and employ them to create new sentences. We write all the statements in our journal.

Employing Writing Practice to Unearth Subconscious Images

As we engage in this word play, we can begin to make metaphors from the material we gathered on the literal level. We take what is linear and literal and draw it out in all directions, playing with the words and phrases to see if we can unearth subconscious images we hold in connection with what is happening. To extrapolate even more information from our literal description, we use something called "writing practice," a technique set forth by teacher and author Natalie Goldman as a way to begin to penetrate subconsciousness and upwell images from that richly complex underworld.[26]

Writing practice (which is always done by writing by hand) has two rules. After determining the length of time during which we will write (beginning with a ten-minute minimum), we must keep our writing hand moving at all times. We are not allowed to stop writing, even if we have to write: "I don't know what to write" or "This is a waste of time" in order to continue moving forward. The second rule is that we are not allowed to go back and cross out; everything that gets put down on the paper stays. We are not permitted to edit with our rational minds which will forbid us to say certain things because of tribal taboos. This censoring function of the rational mind is the part of us that author and astrologer Caroline Casey calls the Reality Police.[27] It is the job of the Reality Police to maintain the status quo. This is a part of our psyche that believes that it keeps us safe by demanding that we follow our inculcated societal and family beliefs about how not to rock the boat, how to stay in denial about things we would rather not deal with and how not to individuate and stray from inherited patterns of behavior. Our goal in writing practice is to not give any attention or authority to the Reality Police, but rather to journey into those places where we are not encouraged to go.

When we first begin writing practice, ten minutes may seem like an eternity; the muscles in our hands may actually begin to ache. However, if we can build up to at least fifteen to twenty minutes or more, we have a better chance of breaking through our very rational, but limiting, mind structures. When this occurs, we may notice that our handwriting actually changes as does the tone and content of what we are writing.

The topics to use for writing practice are the theme of the experience we are trying to decipher symbolically, or any of the circled words or phrases we used in the linear description of the experience. Writing practice can be done many times, using any of the various circled words as a theme, or using the same word or phrase and writing about it each day for a number of days. Or we can circle new words and phrases in our writing practice exercises and use those as the names of our next compositions. Re-reading what we wrote several days later can give us a fresh perspective and new insights about our situation.

What Our Body Says

On the symbolic/metaphorical level, it is also interesting to get physical body responses to the situation we are assessing. We do this by getting quiet, and then paying attention to what happens in our body when we bring the situation into our consciousness.[28] Does the stomach tighten? Do the legs go numb? Is there a churning inside, or maybe an emptiness? Do the eyes itch? Does the jaw freeze? Do the shoulder muscles tense? Is there the feeling of something very heavy on the chest? These are all reactions that we might ordinarily try to ignore or make go away. Instead, we now pay attention to them, and allow ourselves to have the full experience of them, without trying to make them disappear. Then we translate what was happening, including any images that were upwelled during our experience. We keep a record of these translations and add them to our journal.

What happens to us physiologically while we hold a situation in our mind's eye can give us immeasurable insights regarding our reaction or response to the situation we are assessing. Our bodies are meant to be read like sacred text, as the synchronicity of the Bruyere/Cooper steps indicate. Our physicality is an invaluable resource and will point us in the direction we need to go to make conscious buried and outmoded belief systems that are running our lives.

Questions to Ask

An uncomfortable situation in our lives, from mild to severe, usually comes so that we will pay attention to it. The focusing of our awareness on a situation allows us to grow consciously even if we do not intellectually understand what is happening or why. One of the reasons a situation is uncomfortable is because it rocks the boat of our lives; it pulls us out of habitual, numbing patterns, wakes us up and gets us to direct our energy toward a new objective.

Many times we try to maintain the status quo when uncomfortable or painful situations come into our lives. What might be healthier would be to let the situation upset us, notice the ways in which it does and let those upsets metaphorically guide us deeper into ourselves.

To achieve this goal, there is a useful question we can ask: What change in behavior does this event (person, feeling, experience) force upon me?[29] In other words: What does this situation prevent me from doing? and What does this situation force me to do? Looking at the changes in behavior forced upon us by the situation can help us to see just what in our lives might be unsatisfactory that we have not been paying attention to. We will probably notice that the issues that arise out of the situation have arisen before, in either the same way or a similar guise.

Checking for Resonance or Dissonance with Universal Law

It is also helpful to gauge how the situation we are assessing is in harmony or dissonance with universal law. Using our intellect, we evaluate the situation from the perspective of how it follows, or does not follow, the seven basic Universal Laws. It is not so much that we are looking to say, "This situation is out of tune with Universal Laws 3, 4 and 5," but rather that we are examining the problem from a completely different angle than we normally would, one which is energetically based and allows us to explain the dysfunction from an energetic viewpoint. Now, we redefine the situation according to how it resonates with or violates Universal Law. We use the language of Universal Law to write new statements in our journal.

Finding a Central Theme

The journal of writing gained from writing practice and the physical body reactions and images will begin to help us determine the central theme of the situation we are assessing. Re-reading what we have amassed in our journals so far, we look for a common thread woven throughout. We look for an issue, a problem, a statement, phrase or image that pops up again and again. The central theme is always connected to a distorted belief system we are holding and living our lives by, even though it is not serving us. The tentacles of the distorted belief system will have wound their way into many facets of our life.

The central issue may be repeatedly stated as a metaphor or an image. In that case we try to discern and translate the theme of the image/metaphor with regard to our lives. We may find an image repeatedly, but not know what sector of our life it refers to. This is okay. We can carry it with us to the third level for further investigation. As we search for a central issue, it may be helpful to use a dictionary of symbols to help decode our images. These dictionaries explore the symbolism of images and translate metaphors associated with universal archetypes. They can add to the collective pot of our investigation thus far.

Once we are finished with the second level, we realize that we know a great deal more about the original situation than ever before. Now the definition and description of the situation take on much more flavor and are greatly expanded. We are ready to move to the third level: the province of the irrational, non-logical part of us where we take the linear mind out of the driver's seat and put it in the passenger seat in the back of the car.

THE IRRATIONAL/
NON-LOGICAL LEVEL

On the irrational, non-logical level we need to loosen up the tightly-grasped control our personality believes it has on our life. We use the art of meditation and continued writing practice to allow strong images to emerge as we quiet the linear mind. We search for the belief systems related to our situation. We look to see the connection between the outer circumstances of the situation and what is inside of ourselves. We practice being with our bodily experience of being out of harmony with universal law.

Losing Control

On this level, we need to lose the control-based illusion that our personal will is separate from Divine Will. The words irrational and non-logical refer to the idea that we must, to some degree, relax our linear minds and move into an altered state in order to allow our awareness to be led by Divine energies into deeper recesses of our being. This can be a scary thought. Our culture is not one which relies on and pays attention to its dreaming and visions that transcend linear time and space. We are not a society that recognizes or honors our shamans, not yet anyway.

So, if going beyond the parameters of linear thinking seems like a lot of nonsense to us, or if taking a trip closer to subconsciousness is too frightening, we can go no further because the third level of interpretation demands that we turn on our shamanistic lights and venture into powerful realms that have nothing to do with rational, critical thinking.

The intention to go beyond the linear mind must be clearly stated and strongly held to embark upon the journey of the irrational level. If the answers were in our linear minds, we would have found them by now and our problem would be resolved. A situation which is waving a red flag in front of our noses is one which requires that we undertake the hero's journey to venture where we have not gone before. The itinerary involves flushing out our unconscious patterns that reside in the subconscious dimension. We are headed for the altered state where the linear mind does not rule the roost.

Meditating

We move into the third level by upping our writing practice to at least thirty minutes. Again, using our circled words and phrases as the themes, we begin to allow things to come out in our writing that we never would were we stopping to think and edit. What happens as we write, continually moving forward, not crossing out, is that we enter an altered state of objective contemplation, or meditation.

Meditation is the Piscean/Neptunian art of becoming still, quieting the linear mind and training ourselves to focus our attention exactly where we want it to be focused. It is a doorway to the non-rational world because we are no longer listening to "rationality" but quiet enough to hear what is whispered, to find what is full of mystery, to recognize what is underground but really running the show, to discover what is so secret and confidential that even though it is a part of us, we are not privy to it in a linear frame of mind. The fact of the matter is that if we can turn the volume and picture off on the rational mind chatter channel, we can hear and find all sorts of fascinating things tucked away in our psyches.

Of course, as soon as someone says "Meditate," many cry: "I can't do it! And I've tried at least once!" These are the same people who also say "I can't ride a bike/learn to swim/play the piano/do the multiplication tables. And I have tried for five whole minutes!" Practice makes perfect. Some of us are more attuned to meditation the very first time we attempt it; some of us need to practice more; and there will be days when even experienced meditators have trouble focusing. Being able to focus the attention is a very powerful muscle to develop and the Piscean Age has provided us with myriad methodologies, teachers and learning tools. There is also audio technology available now that directs brain wave activity to lead us into alpha, theta and delta frequency states of consciousness.

Whatever the method, the practice of meditation is absolutely crucial to this third step because it allows us entrance to inner worlds. Embodying the archetype of the spiritual warrior, we must go inward to face our dragons and transform those parts of the personality that are keeping us from experiencing all that we really are. This is a necessary part of the healing process and the one we are most likely to resist. We can keep in mind that the story of the hero's journey ends with finding the treasure; this may urge us on.

We can compare a session of meditation to sitting on a quiet riverbank and casting our fishing line into the river.[30] The river is the great water of Universal consciousness, one of Spirit's manifestations which contains everything we need to know. The fishing line thrown into the water is the metaphor for our practice of meditation. We bait the hook on our line with the situation we are assessing, in order to catch the fish that will give us the necessary insights to guide us further on our path. This baiting of the hook is accomplished by holding the situation we are assessing in our consciousness as we enter the altered state.

Just as a fisherman must be patient to catch the fish, so we must be patient as the magnetics of our situation attract to it the guidance from Spirit. The fish we catch may not come to us in linear language. We may catch an image, a metaphor, or better yet, a principle, to steer us to the next step we are to take.

As we still the chattering voice of the linear mind, we are more able to recognize and listen to guidance delivered by Spirit. This comes as an inner voice, a sudden knowing, a fitting together of puzzle pieces in a way that makes sense in our lives. The true inner voice (which is like an e-mail from Spirit) will not flatter or coddle us. It will speak in the language of universal law and point out the spiritual principle with which we need to learn to dance.

Immediately after each meditation session, we should record in our journals any images, insights and guidance that were presented.

The Search for Distorted Beliefs

With a little investigation, we can become aware of some of the distorted belief systems we hold. However, there are others which are deeply buried in subconscious territory. No matter how profoundly entombed our distorted belief systems are, they still run our lives, supplying us with negative thoughtforms and painful emotions which influence our behavior. We create our lives from these ingredients spawned by our distorted beliefs.

The fishing expedition we go on in a meditation session serves to begin the process of digging up the living corpses of our distorted beliefs. This brings them into our waking consciousness. Once we know about them, we can make decisions regarding whether or not we wish to stay attached to them. As we begin to meditate, we can ask for help to notice these negative beliefs.

The excavation of deeply buried beliefs which give us false information about how life works comes many times with the lightning flash of insight; it is not an intellectual exercise. Suddenly we are aware that we have been directing our life according to false laws and erroneous principles. When the illumination of a distorted belief system comes into our consciousness, we usually have a physiological response, ranging anywhere from subtle to grand. It is as if a toxic plant has been uprooted out of our bodies. The sudden rending of what was poisoning us has a physical effect. If the hole left by the uprooted belief is filled with Divine Light, the effect will be more pronounced.

A distorted belief retrieved from the underground cave of our psyche is precious. Its transformation into its positive polar aspect is sacred gold which we find, to our surprise, was our birthright all along.

Bringing the Metaphor into the Third Level

The Law of Correspondence says that whatever we encounter on a small scale, we will encounter on a large scale. The disruption that may be taking place on a cellular level in our bodies can be discerned in our lives, as well. Especially if we are working with the disease process, we will find that the physical symptoms show up in many ways in our daily experiences. Taking our second level metaphor-making into the third level, we construct a visceral graphic of the full circle of ramifications of holding a narrowed view of life.

We can pray for help to be made aware that the discordance we feel in our bodies is also present in our lives and in our environment. We can begin to automatically recognize what previously escaped our notice by actually tuning into the common discordant vibration that has become a theme of our life. Once we know where discord is present, we are free to make choices regarding what to do about it.

When we work with metaphors on the third level, we actively seek kinesthetic awareness of correspondences between dissonance in our bodies and our lives. We focus our intention on picking up subtle physiological, emotional or mental signals that alert us to a thematic "bad vibration." Moving through our day, we are jolted by small recognitions of experiencing the same discomfort, the same frustration, the same deficit, the same confusion or chaos in different areas of our lives — from how illness in our body feels to discomfort created by specific family interactions, to how we feel reading an upsetting story in the newspaper.

This kinesthetic sensing of the metaphors we can make between what happens on inner and outer levels is a non-linear awakening. Something to which we have been desensitized is coming to life, even if that means feeling uncomfortable. Our intuitive faculties rouse us to sensate visceral cues so we can be aware of all the places where the dissonance we are working with exists.

Experiencing Being in Dissonance with Spiritual Law

As we become awakened in such a way, we need to allow ourselves to fully sense how much discomfort and pain our distorted dynamic brings into our lives. When we view life from a limited perspective, not embodying all the power that is available to us as offspring of a Great Force, we are in dissonance with the universe. We are behaving in a manner that does not heed spiritual law.

We have previously discussed how, if we participate in the negative beliefs of mass consciousness, the discomfort of being out of sync with universal law may be numbed by the sheer weight of the magnetics of so many people engaging in the same negative structure. When we want to allow ourselves to feel what it is like to be thrown out of the loving flow of the universe, we must be willing to feel discomfort, realizing that the discomfort is the very thing that mass humanity is trying to avoid feeling. To experience our dissonance, we must become still and quiet, noticing how our energy grates against universal flow.

If we open to It, Spirit will bring us everything we need — on a material level, as well as all others. This universal truth is a challenge for all of humanity to embody. When we cut ourselves off from Spirit, we cause ourselves pain. But if we allow ourselves to experience how painful that separation process is, we are often moved to do something about it.

As we identify discordant resonances throughout our lives, it is extremely beneficial if we step into the dissonance fully. This means allowing ourselves to feel the teeth of the pain we have been avoiding all our lives, moving into it rather than resisting it and hoping it will go away. If we can risk this, we will immediately recognize the bereft despair that our dissonance with Spirit brings. Swimming in these transformational waters for just a *few seconds* can motivate us to move forward in entirely new directions.

We do not need to wallow in our pain, but we do need to know it. Knowing it, we can also know its polar opposite, since they are merely two points on one circular continuum. Knowing it, we can move more easily toward the Light.

THE MEANING/MYSTERY LEVEL

If the third level must be non-linear, the fourth level is even more so. This is a level at which we touch upon Something unexplainable and grand. It is a level of mystery and miracle, a level at which anything at all is possible. It is the level of illumination which we pray for, which brings us understanding beyond the rational mind.

There is no vocabulary to adequately and accurately convey what happens on the fourth level, the meaning/mystery level. On this level, we are no longer operating under any earthly laws of time and space. We have transcended to an awareness of the absolute truth of Spirit, and feel how we fit into the pattern of the universe. Our experience on the earth plane is seen as a thread in a tapestry that is unique to us, while at the same time incorporated into a much larger something that is breathtaking in its simplicity and complexity. Here the language is paradox, the understanding instantaneous. It is the mystery level because it cannot be translated; it is the meaning level because it allows us to come to terms with whatever is happening on the physical plane, giving us a far-reaching perspective and wider eyes with which to see.

On this level, we meditate, we pray, we ask and reach for the mystery. We hold the intention to surrender to the "not-knowing" state of being. We give up trying to control. We instead move into the arms of Spirit and allow the Will-to-Good to direct us. We repeat this behavior over and over, making it a habit. We notice our negative beliefs about how God has abandoned us, how God will not answer our prayers, about how alone and separate we are. We align our intention *not to participate* in these beliefs. We take a risk to name them as illusion and strengthen our faith. We instruct our will not to send any energy to the negative statements. We turn the entire situation over to a Greater Force. We concentrate on opening our hearts in order to access transformational power. We pray some more.

It may be that, reaching this level, we only stay on it for a fraction of a second. That is enough to make a difference. It is this level that aligns our intention to change our lives so that we are living more in accordance with the universal rhythms of Spirit. Not coincidentally, it sometimes comes right after we have experienced the depth of pain which our habitual distorted pattern of behavior brings us.

On this level, we are privy to cosmic patterns in which our lives are moving; we understand the part we are to play. We feel the hand of God in our existence, and in that of all life, and we surrender to Its compassionate touch. We reconnect with the reason we incarnated, and as we do so, we align our lives in accordance with that reason.

The fourth level is an experience of being touched, and thus changed. However we experience it, however vague or clear the experience is, when we emerge from it, we come closer to knowing what it is like to feel whole. This knowing may feel like a dream memory; it may stay completely out of our conscious mind. Or it may reside in our waking consciousness with clarity and distinct images. Whatever the case, the fourth level experience brings us healing, even as it leaves us with responsibilities to move forward in different directions. As we carry the vibration of this healing into our lives, it has the power to renew others in the way that it has renewed us.

THE CREATIVE
PROCESS

◆

ORDERING UP YOUR LIFE

Imagine this scenario. *You receive a hand-delivered invitation offering you a free dinner at a new restaurant in town. The invitation is elegant, the restaurant sounds like a high quality establishment, and you are quite excited with your good fortune.*

That evening you go to the restaurant and as you walk through the doors, you are greeted by the owners, a man and a woman, who welcome you warmly and immediately make you feel at home. You feel like you have known the owners forever, even though you have just met them. They are genuinely delighted to see you and also exceedingly attractive, and they make you feel extremely attractive yourself. You are very glad that you came.

The owners seat you and present you with a menu of astonishing proportion. It seems like its pages go on forever. Before you have a chance to glance at the first page, the owners advise you that this menu contains every meal that you could ever want; however, they are certain that on the very first page of the menu you will find entrées that will particularly delight you. In fact, this first page of the menu has been specialized and personalized just for you. The owners tell you that, because of their admiration and affection for you, it was their intention to offer you precisely what would please you the most. The owners go on to say that of course you can order from anywhere in the menu. It is up to you.

They leave and with excited anticipation, you begin to read the first entrée listed on the first page of the menu. To your delighted amazement, it consists of the foods you absolutely adore, prepared in just the way you are hungry for at that moment. Not only that, but the first entrée comes with the extraordinary guarantee that, if you order this meal, all your relationships will go smoothly for the rest of your life!

There is no doubt in your mind that this is what you will be ordering. But as soon as you make that decision, a little voice pipes up in your head which says: "You must be kidding. That entrée is not for you; it is for someone important and very special." The voice makes you uncomfortable. You squirm in your seat and decide that perhaps you will read on before you make a decision to order.

The second entrée on the first page of the menu again consists of foods you love, prepared in the most appetizing way. In addition, there is a note that states that if you order this dish, you will have financial security for life. You are intrigued and thrilled and you immediately make the decision that this meal will be your dinner order. Once again, as soon as you have made up your mind, a voice in your head begins to speak, this time a little bit louder. "Are you crazy?" it asks. "That entrée is much too pleasurable for you. Who do you think you are to deserve that much pleasure?"

Hearing these remarks, you become unsettled and once again decide to delay your decision about your order. You continue to read the third entrée on the first page and it, like the others, delights you with its promise of culinary enjoyment and the added promise of a lifetime of good health. But the inner voice intrudes once again, and now it is quite loud, telling you that it is impossible that you would be so satisfied and blessed by what is promised.

By now you are very uneasy and decide to see what is in the rest of the menu. You begin to flip through pages, noticing as you do, that the quality of the food decreases with each page you turn. Foods on further pages do not appeal to you nearly as much as what is on the first page.

However, as you read through the entrées, you also notice that the inner voice is much quieter the further back in the menu book you go. In fact, in the second half of the menu, you cannot even hear the criticizing voice at all.

The disappearance of the voice allows you to feel much better, and so you decide that you will order your entrée from a page in the middle of the menu, even though it does not have even half the attraction as the first three dishes listed on the first page. Dessert, though, is a different story. You find that you must choose dessert from the very back of the menu, where the foods are quite mundane and uninspired, in order for the criticizing voice to be quiet.

Once you have made your decision, you call the waiter, who has been quietly standing near your table all this time. Although you have already made up your mind about your order, you ask the waiter a traditional question. Would he recommend anything in particular? The waiter replies: "Oh no. I never recommend, I just take the order. In fact, I really do not have any ideas of my own about ordering." Once you have told the waiter what you would like, he says, "Okay, this order is no problem. I can get this for you. We can get anything at all from the kitchen. This place has great connections."

The waiter brings the order to you and you eat the meal, even though it is of mediocre quality and not exactly what you truly wanted. As you continue to eat, you begin to forget about the first page of the menu, and the fact that the owners specifically told you that you could have whatever you wanted from that page. You begin to accept that the meal you are eating is the best that you can get.

The scenario just described is a good way to begin to understand the creative process and the role we play in it. The phrase "creative process" refers not to our artistic abilities, but to all our daily activities which, if we think about it, all create something. If we wash dishes, we create clean dishes and order in the kitchen. If we yell angrily at someone, we create negative energy and possibly hurt feelings. If we study for a test, we create order in our minds, and an increased ability to focus. We engage in the creative process constantly. It is a human characteristic and our birthright. The problem is we usually are not aware of engaging in it, nor are we aware of how it works and what our dynamics with the process are.

The creative process involves three aspects of our being, which we will call superconsciousness, waking consciousness and subconsciousness. Each of these is represented in the metaphor of ordering in the restaurant.

SUPERCONSCIOUSNESS

The present state of the human mind is so limited in its scope and vocabulary that it can only understand Spirit or God as an abstract concept. Our hearts are actually more able to comprehend what Spirit is by providing us with the ability to feel love. However, there is an aspect of our being which constantly hobnobs with Spirit. We are rarely aware that we have such an asset, such an "in" with the powerful Force that creates and sustains the universe. The part of ourselves which has such a wonderful working relationship with Spirit is called superconsciousness.

The vibratory level of our superconsciousness is far above what is usually manifested in our energy field. It is possible to rev up our frequencies to such a degree that we make contact with the superconscious part of ourselves. However, at the present time we usually do not remain at that high frequency for extended lengths of time.

Superconsciousness is another name for the God Force or Spirit Force that resides within us; we sometimes call it the Higher Self. It is a part of our being that is usually above our conscious awareness. Continually in contact with a Divine Source, superconsciousness is a reflection of the infinite, all-knowing, all-powerful Spirit from which we are birthed. It is the part of us that knows that we have limitless power, derived from our Spirit-source.

Our superconscious Higher Self is always ready to take another step forward. It knows that wherever that step leads us, we will be guided and instructed by Spirit, which will help us interpret our lives in light of our evolving consciousness. Our Higher Self realizes that the movement forward on the path of the evolution of consciousnessis the most pleasurable movement of all.

Our Higher Self adores us and views us with great affection. This superconscious aspect of our being does not condemn us when we make mistakes, but rather is available to steer us on an easier path. It has the ability to guide us through our life, never abandoning us, always supporting us, always ready to lead us on a path of love, joy and pleasure when we are ready. Our superconsciousness knows Spirit is the Will-to-Good which wants the very best for us. From this aspect of ourselves we can view life from a much broadened perspective, aware of Spirit's Greater Plan for our utmost evolvement and fulfillment of our destiny. When we open the energy center at the top of our head, the seventh center, we open the roadway by which we can connect more fully with our superconsciousness and through that aspect, with Spirit.

Because superconsciousness is in constant contact with Spirit, it contains all possibilities because Spirit contains all possibilities. With regard to the creative process, this means that our superconsciousness knows that we can create *anything at all that we want*. There are no limitations; in fact, the vocabulary of our superconsciousness does not include the word "limitation." The superconscious aspect of ourselves is aware of the infinite ways that we can shape our lives. In the restaurant metaphor, superconsciousness is represented by the owners of the restaurant — the male and female in balance, very attractive, delighted to see us, very attuned to exactly what would bring us happiness, and willing to provide us with all possibilities.

WAKING CONSCIOUSNESS

Waking consciousness is our usual state of mind. Members of the human race exhibit myriad stages of waking consciousness, from unevolved to very evolved.

Another name for our waking consciousness is the personality, which contains all our belief systems. Our positive belief systems embrace all possibilities with regard to our creative power; when negative, our beliefs severely limit our possibilities.

The personality is the energy field and as such, it is the vehicle through which we can express Spirit. An unencumbered (undefended) personality allows Spirit to flow through it gracefully. We then radiate Spirit when we speak, think and behave.

The unlimited power and possibilities of Spirit are sent to our waking consciousness by our superconsciousness, which is always in contact with Spirit. When our waking consciousness allows the flow of Spirit through it, we are aware of our unlimited power to create anything we want. When our waking consciousness is riddled with negative beliefs, we impede the flow of Spirit and believe that we are limited as to what kind of life we can create for ourselves. However, let us remember that the energy field, or personality, can be transformed. So we always have the opportunity to recreate our lives in exactly the way we want.

Waking consciousness is actually where the creative process begins. Only waking consciousness can set the wheels in motion which begin to implement our creative power to manifest things, people, events and situations in our life. As we shall see, one of the most powerful tools of our waking conscious minds is that of attention.

Waking consciousness can be compared to Tarot Key 1, the Magician (see *Figure B)*, which shows a young man with his right hand raised. His right hand holds a wand which points upward. The Magician's left hand is pointing down at a garden. The upward direction represents superconsciousness; the garden below represents subconsciousness. The Magician's raised right hand establishes contact with superconsciousness and draws force from it, downward through his body. The left hand points down to the garden of subconsciousness, directing attention to it. The role of the Magician himself is to be a clear channel so that the power and possibilities of Spirit can travel through him to subconsciousness, to make the garden bloom with exactly what he wants.

Notice that without superconsciousness from which to draw power, the Magician would have no creative ability. Superconsciousness provides us with all the resources. If we take it away, we have nothing.

In the restaurant metaphor, waking consciousness is represented by you, the restaurant patron. The critical inner voice is a ramification of negative beliefs held by the patron. In our scenario, the patron was limited in her choice of food by her negative beliefs, even though she was urged by the owners (superconsciousness) to order exactly what pleased her.

FIGURE B: TAROT KEY 1, THE MAGICIAN [31]

1 THE MAGICIAN

SUBCONSCIOUSNESS

Subconsciousness is represented in the restaurant metaphor by the waiter. Completely amenable, ready to get whatever waking consciousness (the restaurant patron) orders, subconsciousness has no ideas of its own. It draws conclusions based on what is presented to it by our waking consciousness. If our waking consciousness believes that there are obstacles to creating exactly what we want, then our subconsciousness believes this also. It *literally* interprets everything sent to it by our waking conscious minds.

The tricky thing about subconsciousness is that it does not readily respond to direct statements. It pays more attention to our emotions, our habits, our thoughts, our expectations, our resistances, our actions, our anxieties and worries, and images in our waking conscious mind. The order in our physical environment sends a message to our subconsciousness, as does any thought, action or emotion we repeatedly run through our systems. Subconsciousness also listens carefully when intense emotion accompanies our feelings, thoughts or actions.

Many times we are unaware of the messages that we send to our subconsciousness. We say one thing, but do another. We desire something, but resist avenues that will begin to create it. We chant affirmations a couple of times, but negate them with our negative images, which we entertain many times a day. If we were able to get a computer printout at the end of each day, listing every statement we made, every thought we had, every image we held, we would probably be quite shocked at what we find. It is a common human trait to focus on what is wrong in our lives, rather than what is right, or what we would like. When we do this, we send messages to subconsciousness, which interprets them as the "order" we are placing for how we would like our life.

When we affirm that we have abundance in our lives, but then obsess all day about how little money is in the bank, subconsciousness interprets that as "I am poor." If we affirm abundance three times a day, and worry about our lack of abundance six times a day, we have told our subconsciousness that we are poor twice as many times as we have told it that we have abundance. Subconsciousness will then assume that we are poor. The abundance message will be completely negated.

The reason we must pay careful attention to what message we send to our subconscious mind, is because, like the waiter, subconsciousness obtains for us what we want. Our subconscious mind, the doorway to which is energetically configured in the sixth energy center, is connected to all points in space. Just as the waiter said, "No problem. I can get that order for you in our kitchen. This place has great connections," our subconsciousness also has great connections with the universal energy field which contains all possibilities.

Every thought we have is an order to subconsciousness to connect us with what we are thinking about. Every resistance, every worry, every repeated activity, places an order with our subconscious mind. Subconsciousness then automatically begins to network for us, finding the same frequency in the universe as we have sent it. So if we obsess about how victimized we are, subconsciousness interprets that as an order for victim experiences, and connects us with just that.

Subconsciousness never has ideas of its own; it will only take orders. It is our waking conscious mind that must change any negative orders to positive ones. We have talked about the filing system that subconsciousness sets up. Every experience is filed in a folder with a specific name. During each day, we are experiencing many things. As we do, we will either support our present filing system, or begin to overhaul certain files. As we worry and think negative thoughts, as we resist change and continue to repeat unhealthy habits, what we are doing is to substantiate a negative filing system already in place. *Subconsciousness will never change the filing system on its own. Only our waking conscious mind has the power to do that.* The filing system creates our life. If we look around us and are not satisfied with certain elements of our life, we must realize that, if we want to, we can recreate those elements so that our life can be the way we would like it to be.

PUTTING OUR CREATIVE
POWER TO WORK

Let us recap the basic working of the creative process. We are connected, through our superconscious self, with Spirit. We have access to tremendous power and all possibilities through this connection. If our waking consciousness is a clear channel, that is, if it is not encumbered with negative beliefs, we can allow the power and possibilities from Spirit to flow through us and send clear messages to our subconsciousness about what we want.

In the restaurant metaphor, the patron was told that she was able to get exactly what she wanted to eat, and more! However, her negative beliefs, coming in the form of a critical inner voice, made her believe that she had limited possibilities for ordering from the menu. She was not willing to risk the discomfort of what would happen if she were to really reach out for what she would like. So she settled for mediocrity and less-than-optimum quality. As she allowed the critical inner voice to have influence over her, she sent a clear order to the waiter about what she wanted. The waiter, representing the subconscious mind, simply said, "Okay, I can get that for you," and then went to the kitchen, which was connected with all points in the universe, and ordered up exactly what the patron had said. The patron was served with mediocrity when she really desired the very best! As she eats her meal, she walls off the knowledge that she could have had something that exactly matched her desire.

If we study this scenario, we can see that our point of power is in the waking conscious mind. Superconsciousness is simply there; it is our birthright as we come into a human body. Subconsciousness is part of the package also, and merely waits to do our bidding. However, the waking conscious mind, the one we use every day, is the only place where we have some control. We can direct our waking consciousness in whatever way we wish.

Let us look again at Tarot Key 1, the Magician. There is a table to the Magician's left and on it are four implements. These are tools that assist the Magician in the creative process. We see a wand, a cup, a sword and a coin.

The wand represents attention. The Magician must focus his attention on exactly what it is he wants to create. This is like sending a strong beam of energy towards a goal. The energy brings the goal to life. The Magician uses his will to direct his attention towards his goal.

The cup represents the Magician's memory and imagination. Memory refers to the filing system in the sixth energy center where we keep the memory of every experience filed away under a certain heading. In order to be a clear channel, the Magician must make sure that the names on the file folders are not impediments to the flow of energy through him from superconsciousness. Only the Magician has the power to change the names on the file folders by redefining all his experiences in the light of how they have helped him evolve, rather than on how they have hurt him.

The Magician uses his imagination to produce a mental image of what it is he wants to create. Images are powerful messages to the subconscious. As the Magician creates an image, he actually arranges his energy field to be able to accept from superconsciousness the exact frequency which matches the image. He either becomes a vessel which is better prepared to allow the unlimited power and possibilities of Spirit to flow through him, or he structures his energy so that it blocks Spirit from coming in.

The sword on the table represents action. Action means the steps the Magician must take that move him closer to manifesting what he wants to create. This would include actions that change negative belief names in the subconscious filing system to positive belief names. Action also means that the Magician must actively feel his desire to create his goal, and allow his longing and yearning to help carry the creative energy coming through from superconsciousness.

The coin is the finished product, the urge to create manifested into form. If we look at the coins on our own table, and they are not to our liking, we need to employ the Magician's other tools to recreate our life.

STEPS FOR THE CREATIVE PROCESS

I. Make a Target

If we want to create something, we have to know exactly what it is we want to create. If we are aiming the arrow of our concentration toward a target, we need a clearly defined one or we will never hit the bulls-eye. So the first step in the creative process is defining a specific target by answering the question "What do I want?"

We need one sentence that clearly states our goal. It must be specific, not vague. It should not contain the name of another person, since we have no control over the choices of anyone else.

When we first write our goal-statement, we should sit with it for several days, re-evaluating it each day to see if it states exactly what we want to create. The language we use is very important. Any vagueness or imprecision may bring results we are not expecting. There is the much-told story of the woman who set as her goal the statement: "I want a husband." Following through with the creative process, she found that other women's husbands became very interested in having a relationship with her.

Our goal-statement should also be written without negatives. We need to state what we *want*, not what we *do not want*.

When we evaluate our goal-statement, we need also to evaluate our *intention* toward carrying it out. Sometimes we might say what we think we should want, but are actually afraid of the changes that would come if we attained the objective. In order for the creative process to work, it must be anchored by firm intention. That includes dealing with the ramifications of achieving the goal. If the intention is not strong, we will falter in our creation, because unconsciously we do not really want to attain the goal at all.

2. Believe You Have the Power to Create

If we see our goal-statement as a fantasy that will never come true, that is exactly what will happen. If we believe that we are not powerful enough to create the life we want, we will manifest just that. We derive our power from Spirit, and as long as we keep Spirit energy flowing from our superconsciousness, we have an infinite amount of power, far beyond what the average human manifests today.

The power to create is part of our birthright. If the belief in that power is missing from our filing system of beliefs, we need to address the deficit. We need to take the risk that it just might be true that we are powerful creative beings. What have we got to lose?

3. Use the Words "I Am" with Care

The most powerful words in the English language are the words "I am." Together with the words that follow, they produce a potent force that has the power to create exactly what we say. Our subconsciousness perks up immediately when it hears the words "I am," and listens attentively to how we complete the sentence. We need to remember that any sentence that begins with these words will have a more powerful impact than other statements.

Any words that follow "I am" should be words that define us as children of God and carriers of Divine Light, and the birthright that springs from that. Even if we do not *feel* that this is true, it really is. Any other belief is an illusion of separation. Any statement that contradicts this concept supports negative belief systems that will create our life accordingly.

4. Create an Image

If we cannot imagine what we want, we will not be able to create it. Imagining our goal is like making a mold that will hold the energetic configurations of what we want. *These configurations must be in place in our energy field for our goal to manifest.*

Creating an image involves some conscious dreaming. We picture in our mind's eye what life would be like if our goal *were already a reality*. We add sensory images to make it more real — colors, sounds, textures, smells. We put ourselves in the picture and imagine what it would feel like to have already attained our goal. It is beneficial to get very specific in this regard. If, for example, we have as our goal-statement: "I want to be recognized as the valuable employee that I am, and compensated for the full value of my worth," we might imagine the respect we receive from our bosses, as well as how we would feel on payday as we look at the increased amount on the paycheck. We could imagine depositing the check in our bank, adding up our new balance, and so forth. The color of the check, the way it feels in our hands, the congratulatory remarks of our co-workers, the delight of our family — all these are specific details which makes our imagery stronger and more real.

It is important to see our image as a present reality. If we see an image that is in the future, that is what we will create. We will always be a few steps away from it, instead of having in our present life. Holding an image of our goal-statement as a present reality charges our image in our energy field with manifesting power.

5. Desire What You Want; Link Desire with The Heart

We can liken the creative process to the act of shooting an arrow at a target, trying to hit the bulls-eye. One of the things that urges us to fit the arrow to the bowstring in the first place is the force of desire.

Desire and the will work hand in hand. Residing together in the fifth energy center, our desire is a catalyst for our will energy to get to work. The stronger our desire, the more chance that the will will begin to direct energy toward the object of our desire.

Strong desire is a great impetus in the creative process. It is important to allow ourselves to feel the longing and yearning we have with regard to our goal, to let ourselves feel that magnetic pull urging us toward what we want. When our desire is aligned with heart energies, its force becomes even more magnificent.

For example, a friend of mine really loved the water and wanted to live in a house where he could see the water from his bedroom window. Every time he drove by a creek or stream or lake in his neighborhood, he allowed himself to feel how pleasurable it was for him to be near the water. He let himself be delighted and awed by the sight of water. He felt the soothing caress of its sound. He raptured in the way the sight of water lit him from within. He visited places by bodies of water and breathed in the smells, enjoying every minute, letting himself feel the pleasure that being near water brought him. He spoke aloud to himself about how he longed to be able to delight in the sensate emanations of water every morning when he woke up. He spoke of his desire every time he was near the water by saying, "I really, really *love* the water." He let his jaw drop, felt his upper chest being tugged by his yearning, and allowed his heart center to open up as he experienced his love for the water. All of this sent strong and loud messages to his subconscious mind, which could not miss just what it was the man was ordering. Two weeks after he began working with his desire in such a way, the man found his dream — an affordable house on a beautiful lake.

When desires are linked with the heart, they take on a sacred energy. Anything touched with the quality of love is rendered holy. If we can open our hearts as we feel our desire, we sanctify our longing. Sometimes the heart energy changes the desire to some degree; sometimes it even completely replaces it. In any case, what we find is that the energy of love purifies our desires in such a way that they become part of our heart's desire, our longing. Our longing represents our task, the reason that we incarnated. Healer, teacher and author Barbara Brennan teaches that once our personal task has been completed, it is transformed into our world task, a way that we can help to heal the planet. When our desire is transformed in some way by the energy of love, we find that the transformed desire is even more of what we want.

We sometimes feel desire that is not at all aligned with our hearts. Consciously or unconsciously, we can manifest these desires through the creative process. However, desire isolated from the heart has its own consequences, not the least of which is that it pulls us off the path of our true destiny on detours which can be quite time- and energy-consuming, as well as painful. The best way to work with desire is to feel it as we open our hearts. We open the heart by thinking of some part of life that we love. When the energy from the fourth center and the energy from the fifth center have lines of open communication, when their frequencies harmonize, we will feel it and know that we are on the right track.

6. Dismantle the Secret Codes

Sometimes we consciously use the creative process and it seems that the results that we get are the opposite of what we want. This can be very frustrating. However, it is an opportunity to learn more about ourselves as we become more scrupulous about the messages we send to our subconsciousness.

When we place an order with our subconsciousness, it immediately begins to network for us to connect us with the exact magnetics that we are sending out. It is as if we hand subconsciousness an energetic package, which from the outside, may look very nice and exactly like what we say we want. However, if the creative process is not working, it simply means that we have hidden in the package some energetic "secret codes" which may negate other energetic configurations and bring a completely different set of magnetics to the order we give our subconscious.

We are usually not conscious of these secret codes. If we are, we have the choice to do something about them. But it often is the case that the package we hand to our subconscious contains energetic configurations of negative belief systems of which we are not aware.

The best way to work with this opportunity is to take a look at our life and see what part of it brings us discomfort or pain. We may want to use the four-step method of symbolic interpretation to gain more insight about what is happening. Some belief systems, especially those which have been programmed in us as small children, feel like they are simply part of who we are, and we are not likely to even think about their existence. We simply let them run our lives.

We need to be aware of just what our belief systems are. We need to be familiar with the negative beliefs which will not only challenge what we want, but also negate it. Everyone has negative beliefs yet to be transformed. The unearthing of unconscious belief systems is very important.

If, for example, we are working on creating abundance, and it seems that we just keep getting poorer, it means that there are deeply ingrained beliefs about abundance that we now have the opportunity to work with. One of the first places we should check is the daily review of the images regarding abundance that we have created, the thoughts about abundance we have had, the words we have spoken regarding it, and so forth. It is very common to focus on what we do not have, rather than what we have; on what is wrong with our life, rather than what is right. This is a human trait, which we can turn around with our attention and focus.

If we can be curious about what is going on with our messages, rather than self-judgmental or impatient, we can partake of a great opportunity for more clarity and insight. In the long run, a "secret code" can give us more of ourselves.

7. *Surrender to the Universe*

We usually have a big investment in having life turn out the way we want it to. We have our desires, and our images of what we want, and when our scenario does not appear, we feel angry, hurt, rejected, dismayed and frustrated. We have "followed the steps" and "done the work," and life is not happening according to our plan. We demand to know "Why, why, why" things are happening as they are.

In our moments of greatest frustration in not being able to get what we want, we need to let go of our insistence that things happen exactly the way we think they should. Accepting our lives as they are does not mean that we are "giving in," collapsing or losing. It does mean that we begin to work with what is, to make the most of it, to learn the most from it, to come to terms with our human condition. This is an act of surrender which allows us to flow with the Divine Plan that is constructed by the Will-to-Good, to bring us to a level of joy and satisfaction that at the moment we cannot comprehend.

If we second-guess how the Universe is guiding us, we are in disharmony with life. Conversely, if we collapse and give up, we are also in disharmony with life. Surrendering to the Universe means that we say to Spirit: "What is it you would have me do?" If our road takes a turn that we did not expect, we accept what is and continue to work with our experiences in order to see them as the invaluable classrooms of opportunity of our time on this planet.

Being willing to give up the attachment to what we have decided would be the very best thing for us can be difficult. If we pray as we let go, the space we create by giving up our investment in the outcome of events is filled with the force of Spirit. When this happens, we know we are supported in our forward movement, even if it looks very different from what we thought it would be.

Surrendering to the Universe means letting go of the belief that our will, our personality, can exist without flowing in the river of Divine Will. It makes us redefine our humanness and realize that we exist *because* of a great Power which creates and sustains all life.

CONSCIOUS USE OF
OUR CREATIVE POWER

We use the creative process constantly, but we are usually not aware of doing so. We are actually extremely practiced in using the creative process. However, we are amateurs when it comes to using it consciously. Let us remember that to be proficient at something, we usually have to consciously practice certain techniques or exercises. Each time we practice we gain more control over our ability to focus; in the practicing, we become more familiar with ourselves, gaining understanding of how we have a tendency to operate, and what needs adjustment.

The same is true of the creative process. Using it consciously is an Aquarian Age lesson; the urge will be present to become more aware of how the creative process works and how we work with it. As we practice and learn, we will regain more and more of our true selves.

To gauge what kind of order you place with your subconscious mind, think back over your day and answer these questions.

+ What did you say you wanted today? What did you wish for? Do those statements define an appropriate goal?

+ What did you imagine today? Wonderful things for your

life or the continuation of stress? Positive pictures to increase your joy and pleasure or negative scenarios that you really would like out of your life?

✦ What did you desire today? Good things for you? Bad things for someone else? Or were you self-judging, desiring the worst to happen to you, so you could prove that your negative beliefs about yourself were true?

✦ What kind of orders did you place with your subconsciousness today? Did you pay attention to what was right with your life or what was wrong? Did you once focus on how you would like your life to be? What was the ratio of positive images, feelings, thoughts, desires and actions to negative ones?

✦ What was the overall message your subconsciousness got from you today?

THE HEART OF
THE MATTER

AQUARIUS' DEMAND
FOR A STRONG HEART

For the past two thousand years, the presently waning Age of Pisces has urged us to explore the power of the heart and its alchemical energies of love, compassion and forgiveness. These qualities of the fourth energy center are the ingredients for the medicine which will heal the pain of our planet; they are absolutely essential in order to fulfill the demands of the Aquarian Age.

One of the mandates we are given by the new age is to perfect our relationships and to create a world community. If we neglect to put our hearts into the relationships and communities we create, the result will be the disaster that encompasses much of the world today. A relationship which does not contain the energy of love and compassion is sure to be uncomfortable or painful. Love and compassion engender respect and dignity, and if these are missing in any type of relationship, resentment and anger will breed.

If we want to participate in the creation of a healthy global community, we must begin at home, with our own relationships. *Every single person* with whom we enter into relationship is our teacher, and can be a catalyst for us to find ways to live in harmony, peace and beauty with others. As Aquarian energy pushes us to acknowledge and feel our inherent interconnectedness and relationship with every other person on the planet, and with all forms of life, we begin to realize that what we must bring to this interconnectedness is the strength of the heart that was to be developed during the Piscean Age. The heart immediately transforms the way we behave and think, not only with respect to our close relationships, but also with respect to mass humanity. The heart energies of love and compassion bless what we send through the energetic passageways that connect us with all of life. Having the ability to keep our heart open in all our relationship dynamics will raise the vibration of the energy we send through the universal energy net. Needless to say, our world can use every bit of higher vibration we can radiate.

We have talked about the fourth energy center being the center that processes our beliefs about relationships. The physical heart, with its septum-divided halves brought together as one powerful organ, is a metaphor for the perfect relationship, an Aquarian desire. The heart's four chambers must work in perfect harmony for the heart to perform its job of pumping blood throughout the body via the circulatory system. When the physical heart does its job well, it has the extraordinary ability to pump four to five liters of blood *every minute*, even though the total blood volume of an average person is only five to six liters. When the energetic heart does its job well, it has the extraordinary ability to pump acts of kindness and compassion all over the globe. *One person* can be the source of a planetary movement toward healing.

WHAT IT MEANS TO
HAVE AN OPEN HEART

If the physical heart seems like a wondrous creation, the energetic heart, with its loving, compassionate properties, is even more so. As the Heavenly Alchemist, the energetic heart can transform the crudest energy into wealth and riches. We exhibit this potential when we first fall in love and allow ourselves to be altered in a very positive way. Our defenses and worst behaviors can abate, and we are able to exhibit a fineness and openheartedness that last as long as our eros does. In the same way, the energy of love and compassion has the ability to transform and heal any situation in our lives. Remember that the energetic heart center is the place where the way we feel about and define an experience has the opportunity to be transformed. If the heart is open, that is, if we allow energy to move fully through it, it has the power to allow the sacred gold of any experience to emerge.

A person with an open heart allows the free flow of emotional energy throughout the energetic heart center. She *is willing to feel*, whether the feeling be joy or grief. Feelings move in waves, and will pass through our energy field, rather than remain forever. It is when we attempt to resist feelings that we do not allow them to move. Then they become stationary. The willingness to allow ourselves to have feelings is one of the first steps in creating a healthy, open heart center. This can sometimes seem quite risky because of beliefs we hold about how feelings can hurt, and even destroy us. However, in opening the heart to allow feelings to flow, we also open it to its core of invincible strength, harmony and peace. These qualities *cannot be accessed* if we close our energetic hearts in an attempt not to feel. They will remain dormant, unused and unattainable just when we need them the most.

We must remember that the heart is magical. No other part of our being has the alchemical power to turn something which feels painful or chaotic into a deep peace and serenity. When we are willing to open the heart, the energies of love and compassion are mixed into the flow of feelings. As these natural components of the heart are mixed with whatever emotions are flowing through the heart center, they temper the mixture and upwell the inner core qualities mentioned. The allowance of the flow will affect the entire body, and the qualities in the core of every energy center will be ignited.

The open heart gives us the ability to sense what is beneath inappropriate behavior. It recognizes the pain and the profound forgetting of our magnificence which spurs every negative action, word and thought. In this recognition, we feel our universal humanity and are flooded with the understanding of our interconnectedness. The relationship between the other person and us immediately deepens intimately, and our intention is aligned to be of support, solace and comfort in helping the other feel love, compassion and forgiveness for him or herself. When these resonances are present, our response to the person is immediately aligned with the strong magnetics of universal law. Then our forward movement is supported by the universe. The right road opens up before us and we make the most appropriate choices.

There is confusion and much mis-education in our society about what it means to have an open heart. There are misguided beliefs that if our heart is open, we cannot make comfortable boundaries for ourselves, or we must condone inappropriate behavior. This is not true. In recognizing the pain of another and connecting more intimately with the person, we experience our common Spirit and the love it engenders for ourselves, for others and for all of life. When our hearts are open, we also may need to set limits, and we always need to honor and take care of ourselves. We hold everyone accountable for his or her thoughts, words and deeds. The universe, acting through the Law of Cause and Effect, will set wheels in motion by which everyone will experience the consequences of his or her behavior, consequences that are an impetus to transform inner pain.

So open-hearted people are willing to feel and to relate deeply with another. At the same time, they will not allow inappropriate behavior to continue and will set the strong boundaries that are needed so that the behavior does not impact themselves or others in a negative way. The way that open-hearted people hold their energy creates a strong magnetic force which will have an effect on the other person. Just what effect that will be cannot be predicted. The magnetics of an open heart may throw a misbehaving person into a rage, because it urges the misbehaving person to allow his or her own feelings to move. Or the misbehaving person may be able to accept the harmonious, loving energy of an open heart and find solace in it. We have no control over what another will do with energy we send; we only have control over what we radiate.

When we have an open heart, we feel more, and this means we feel more grief as well as joy. The universal Law of Rhythm demands that the pendulum swing will be equal between both sides. We have to be willing to allow the painful emotions to flow, just as we do the pleasurable ones. The more we open our hearts, the more we open to the pain of the world, and this is so immense and overwhelming that sometimes we simply must lie down and weep. However, again, this is a *movement through* the heart center, not a permanent state. Ancient wisdom teaches that it is possible to lift oneself up into a higher vibration when the pendulum swing is toward the very painful end of the continuum. In doing so, we still feel, and still feel pain, but the sharpness of it is tempered.

FOCUSING HEART
ENERGIES INWARDLY

One of the reasons that we are so transformed by the eros of a new relationship is because, in addition to falling in love with someone else, we also fall in love with ourselves. As we receive affection and love and admiration from another person, it helps us to open to our own capacity to love, admire and be affectionate toward ourselves. Even a small amount of love turned inward can have a tremendous effect on our lives. The transformational powers of love, compassion and the ability to forgive are not only for others; they are also meant to be focused on us.

The heart energies contain the energies of *self*-love, *self*-compassion and *self*-forgiveness. The challenge begins right here. We are much more prone to be able to give out these qualities than to take them in for ourselves. We are not talking about being overly indulgent with ourselves, or narcissistic. Balance is always what we strive for. But to be powerful, our heart centers must be able to be as loving, compassionate and forgiving towards ourselves as we are towards others. We need to be strong at both ends of the spectrum.

To love ourselves may seem like the most confusing task. Especially when we have not had much experience of being loved, we may feel that we do not know the first thing about how to love ourselves. However, we are all given the birthright of Divine Love, the never-ending, unconditional compassion that comes to us from Spirit. We have all experienced such love, whether or not we remember it. There is never a time when we are separated from Spirit and Its infinite love for us. The illusion of the human condition is that we believe such separation exists. It is our responsibility as evolving beings, to search for the understanding that lets us know that the love that is Spirit is with us always.

Taking Marriage Vows to Ourselves

Teacher, author and medical intuitive Dr. Caroline Myss has associated the sacrament of marriage with the fourth energy center of the heart.[32] To begin the healing and empowerment of any energy center, we apply the sacrament to ourselves first. Using this symbolism, we can begin to practice upwelling love for ourselves by working with the statements that reflect the grace which the sacrament of marriage bestows upon the individuals in a marriage ceremony.

Let us use the following three statements regarding the traditional sacrament of marriage:

1. **Marriage is a sacred pledge of devotion to the other.**
2. **Marriage is about fidelity — being true to the other.**
3. **Marriage bestows an ability to resist the temptation to abandon the other, despite the hardships that might cause.**

To understand the healing of the heart center as first requiring a partnership, or marriage, with ourselves, we can substitute the word "myself" for the phrase "the other." Because the word "marriage" is a metaphor for healing the heart, we can also substitute the phrase "healing my heart" for the word "marriage." Now we have three statements that read as follows:

1. **Healing my heart is a sacred pledge of devotion to myself.**
2. **Healing my heart is about fidelity — being true to myself.**

3. Healing my heart bestows an ability to resist the temptation to abandon myself, despite the hardships that might cause.

If we read the statements aloud, in order to *feel* their energy, we realize that they are very powerful. Together they connote a vow of love, fidelity and steadfastness made to ourselves. This means being as tender and forgiving toward ourselves as we would be to someone we love and cherish. We remember to praise ourselves. We take the time and care to make sure the words we use to speak to ourselves are positive, rather than negative, even when we are noticing where we need to change our behavior. We do not put ourselves down or call ourselves names. We are very careful with what words follow the phrase "I am."

The revised statements are about being true and faithful to ourselves in the way that we are to loved ones. We resist the temptation to abandon ourselves and forget our birthright to be loved. We take the risk of staying connected with ourselves, even when we are experiencing unpleasant or frightening emotions. Being faithful and loyal to ourselves can be a risk, because in order to do so, we may have to risk a "negative" reaction from another person. This kind of "hardship" that may be the result of not abandoning ourselves must be endured if we are to open our heart.

The concept of self-love does not relieve us of behaving responsibly; we always need to acknowledge the consequences of our actions, words and attitudes. However, in order to have a strong heart center, we must treat ourselves with kindness and consideration, remembering that our soul is no less the reflection of Spirit as anyone else's. Just as we would attempt to teach a child right from wrong without harsh criticism which can injure, we are careful with our thoughts and our speech when pointing out to ourselves where we have room for improvement.

These behaviors need to be practiced. Some of us did not have a model for how to treat ourselves kindly and with love. However, since we are birthed from Spirit and it is the nature of Spirit to have a full heart, it is also our inherent nature to have a full heart. We are capable of devotion to ourselves and it is our responsibility to break old patterns that foster negativity, rather than love, toward ourselves.

Forging a partnership with ourselves is a prerequisite to a healthy heart center. It is through the energetic heart center, as well as the crown center, that we connect with that aspect of our being we call our Higher Self, that part of us that realizes we are in continuous contact with Divine Spirit. This connection is a lifeline when we face crisis and pain.

A TIME OF CHANGE
AS A TIME OF TESTING

There is another reason that we will need our hearts open and strong in the Aquarian Age. As we move into the evolutionary cycle of a new astrological age, we can be sure that we will be urged to transform our beliefs about how life works. In the past, humanity has had difficulty with the changes a new age can bring. Right now we are in a crucial interface period with the energy of the waning Piscean Age bursting forth strongly while at the same time we are feeling more deeply the impact of the energy of the Water Bearer.

The movement from one evolutionary cycle into another is always a time of increased testing. We are tested on the lessons of the waning age to see if we have integrated them. Simultaneously, we are tested to see if we are willing to allow what we have just learned to evolve. We are also tested to see where we stand with regard to the lessons of the new age. These tests show up in small ways in our day-to-day life *and they always involve opening our heart more fully*. Not paying attention to these small tests is to invite larger, more arduous trials.

Every test, large or small, is an opportunity to grow consciously as we strengthen our hearts. Trials are actually the way Spirit cares for us, guides us and loves us by moving us through life on a path of evolving consciousness. This path leads to our destiny, the reason for which we incarnated. Our destiny is the longing of our heart and soul. Fulfilling it brings to our life the greatest sense of contentment and balance that is possible. The Will-to-Good, wanting the very best for us, wanting us to fulfill our destiny and have the utmost contentment and balance, gives us trials to keep us on the right road. Although the trials we experience may be painful, they are actually gifts which can bring us great riches if we view them with a sense of surrender to a Higher Power. We can complain and whine about our trials, or we can accept that they are a way that Spirit uses to help us become the powerful creative being we are meant to be. The first perspective makes life difficult. The second makes it easier.

Let us use a metaphor to understand this. Suppose that you are a member of a sports team. As you practice, your coach watches you carefully and gives you guidance as to what skills you need to work on. The coach may push you to go farther than you think you can. She may seem relentless with respect to what is expected of you. When you listen to the coach, when you apply yourself and focus on practicing and perfecting your skills, your performance gets better and better. It becomes easier for you to play the game; you move with confidence and grace and balance. Even though your coach continues to push you to improve, you understand that it is with the intention to help you move through the game with ease. You experience the satisfying consequences of your hard work, *even though the work itself may not be pleasant.* You feel very secure that your coach will point out to you where you need to focus. This makes you more confident because you know that someone is looking out for you. You realize that the coach only wants you to do your best and feel good about it.

Your coach purposely puts you in situations where you are tested and challenged to go beyond your present level. You know that you can pass the tests if you remember the instruction and guidance from your coach, and if you focus and practice. You realize that the tests will make you a better player and you welcome the challenge. Even when you "fail" a test, you realize that it helps you to notice where you need to focus. You understand that every test, whether you pass it or not, allows you to grow.

When you refuse to accept guidance from your coach, your performance falters. The game becomes more difficult, and you feel that it is a continuous test which you constantly fail. You feel that your coach is mean, has it in for you and only wants to harass you. You do not want to know about your shortcomings; you do not want to apply yourself to the work that is needed to improve. It all seems too troublesome and painful and you want no part of it. Consequently, playing on the team becomes unpleasant and difficult.

We can think of Spirit as the coach who wants the best for us, and is willing to pay specific, careful attention to us in order to help us become the player we would love to be. If we can be willing to listen to and be guided by Spirit, we can reach the top of the mountain, and reach it much more easily than if we refuse direction or think we have to go it alone. Spirit tests us continually, but it is a way of helping us move in the right direction, along our personally individualized path toward fulfillment of our task. If we allow our hearts to be open to our connection with Divine Force, our response to life's tests will boost our inner Spirit, and we will realize that life is a continuous miracle. We will also feel supported and secure in the knowledge that Something greater than we are is guiding us moment by moment.

Closing our hearts to Spirit is like disregarding our coach's guidance. It is not believing that Spirit constantly provides an impetus for us to move toward exactly what will fulfill us the most. We always have a "coach," whether or not we acknowledge it. To believe that we can be separate from that coach we call Spirit brings us great pain and can be the source of much anger. When we hold that separation belief we distort the energy in both our seventh energy center and our heart center.

In esoteric Tarot, Key Number Fourteen is called the Intelligence of Probation and is associated with the energetic heart. Probation means a time of testing and trial not only to determine, but to support, our wholeness. It consists of precise, significant examinations and assessments. These examinations are administered by Spirit in the form of challenges to our status quo, what we might call initiations. Whatever form they come in, we can be sure that they are exactly what we need in order to be able to attain the most growth of consciousness. *Our ability to pass our initiatory tests depends on the strength of our heart centers, and how well we can upwell the energies of love, compassion and forgiveness.*

The picture on Key Fourteen is of the archangel Michael who represents the guiding, protecting, loving Spirit that is always with us. The angel also represents the Heavenly Alchemist, transforming what is base into something beautiful. This is the potential of our heart center which is perfected through the tests we are given by Spirit. Through our trials we are able to create gold through the power of our hearts, meaning we bring to our life the precious, priceless gifts of love, compassion and forgiveness, both for ourselves and for the world.

The 1999 winter issue of *Spirituality & Health* magazine related a story which gives us the proper perspective with regard to the heart. The Dalai Lama, spiritual leader of Tibet, told about a friend of his who had spent almost twenty years in Chinese labor camps. His friend told him that during the time he was imprisoned, he had sometimes faced real danger. When the Dalai Lama asked him what kind of danger, he replied, "The danger of losing compassion for the Chinese."[33]

Because we are in the transition stage between two ages, the tests and trials we face may be more demanding of us than at other times. We must realize that the true dangers for ourselves, individually, and as a planet, lie not in the tests themselves, but in keeping our hearts closed. If we do not focus on opening our hearts, we may be lost in the Forest of Thorns for a very long time.

A STORY TO EXPERIENCE
THE POWER OF THE HEART

Imagine yourself in the following situation in which we will explore how you would respond to a certain stressful experience. Although the intention here is to give you an opportunity to have the visceral sensation of your heart opening, we will also be reviewing the way in which an experience travels through the seven centers of the energetic body.

Here is the scenario. You are in the parking lot of the grocery store, carrying several bags of groceries to your car when one of the bags rips and your groceries spill out all over the lot. You attempt to pick up your spilled groceries while holding onto the other bags. Cans and bottles are rolling away from you, you drop your car keys, and the whole scene is very frustrating.

A man driving an old pick-up truck is attempting to pull out of the lot, but now has to stop and wait while you scurry around trying to collect everything, which seems to be taking a long time. The driver of the truck begins honking his horn impatiently, which only serves to make you more agitated, and a glass jar of juice drops from your hands and smashes on the asphalt. The driver of the truck, seeing the broken glass, leans out his window and yells some derogatory comments your way.

You look up and see that there is now a line of cars waiting to pull out of the lot, and you attempt to hurry to pick up the broken glass and put it in one of the unbroken bags. Of course, this delays the clean-up process even more, and finally, the driver of the truck really loses it and screams and curses at you out of his window. He then guns his engine, pulls around you so closely he barely misses hitting you and, tires squealing, exits the parking lot.

Stop for a moment and allow yourself to enter that drama. Let it play out with your own habitual reactions or responses. Be truthful about how you would behave in such a situation. Be willing to let yourself *feel* how you would react.

Now let us look at what is happening to your energy field as you go through this experience. The energy of the event comes in through your first energy center, which will define the experience based on how safe you feel, how supported, and how much you have embodied the concept that all existence comes from one Source. If the first center is healthy, this definition is a simple statement of what happened, a statement that does not pit the driver of the truck against you. However, if your first energy center holds negative beliefs about the unity of existence, those beliefs will color your definition of the event and something much different will be produced. The driver of the truck cursed and screamed at you and drove his truck dangerously close to you, and these actions may make you define the experience as an encounter with an enemy who wanted to hurt you. You feel unsafe, your sense of stability is shaken, and you define the event in the framework of a "me versus them" consciousness that immediately throws you out of resonance with the universal Law of One. When you are out of resonance with the universe, it is quite a heavy burden, and only serves to make you feel worse and react more negatively.

Depending on your habitual defensive reactions to the establishment of an enemy, you now may want to run and hide, cry, whine, blame, scream and curse, or go after the guy and teach him a lesson. It depends on how your second energy center interprets the event. The second center is programmed to deal with how powerful you feel you are, and it will immediately generate an emotional feeling connected with your beliefs about your power in this situation. You may believe that the man in the truck was trying to overpower you, and you will have a habitual behavioral pattern that emerges because of that belief. You may feel powerless and want to collapse. You may feel your power threatened and want to threaten back in retaliation. The question you are asking yourself, either consciously or unconsciously, at this point is: "Who has more power right now? Am I on the top rung of the power ladder, or is the driver of the truck on a rung above me, and what can I do about it?"

This is a great opportunity for your victim energy to be awakened, and it may make a statement like: "The driver of the truck is a bad man. If only he had not done that, I would feel better. I was powerless to defend myself against such an angry person." A more aggressive interpretation would be to decide that this guy has to be taught a lesson, and you are just the one to do it. You will show him who has more power, even if it is just in talking about the situation over and over, and proving to others how victimized you were. This makes you right and the man wrong. This belief provides a pretty strong white horse to ride up into the third energy center. There, you will use it to prove that you are "good."

Perhaps you have done some self-awareness work and are secure in your beliefs about your power, in which case you will view the event in a more objective manner. You do not even consider the question of who has more power, since you are well aware that everyone has the same infinite supply. From this perspective, you know that your job is not to establish an enemy camp, no matter what behavior someone is exhibiting. *This does not mean you condone the driver's behavior.* It does mean that you are not afraid that the driver has the power to take away your power, and you do not need to spend any energy on "getting power over" the driver before he "gets power" over you. If your second energy center beliefs are this healthy, your first emotional response to the incident will not include helplessness, anger or a need for revenge. Instead, you respond with feelings of calmness, centeredness and strength.

If your third energy center is healthy, the opinions and thoughts about the event which are processed there, will read something like this: "I am worthy of respect and dignity from myself and everyone else. I will not take on as truth anything the driver said about me. I know I am okay. I can choose to set boundaries for myself so that I do not have to be around people who do not show me respect." In this case, your healthy sense of yourself allows you to know that you are okay and not bad. You also know that your worth is not dependent on what someone else says, and that you are capable of taking care of yourself.

Compare this to the opinions and thoughtforms that come out of the distorted third energy center: "What if the things he said are true? Why didn't he like me? What did I do wrong? Maybe it is my fault that he got angry. How should I have behaved so I did not displease him or make him angrier? What is wrong with me?" Or you may think: "I must prove that I am good by making him really bad." The unhealthy third energy center allows your self-worth to be called into question by the remarks of a stranger. It might coerce you to spend a lot of time and energy "proving" that you were the "good one" in the scenario.

Take a moment to recap where you are right now. Which statements ring true for you? How would you be feeling if you were a player in the parking lot drama? Does it remind you of similar incidents in your life?

Now we move to the fourth energy center, that of the heart. A healthy heart center would be feeling compassion and forgiveness for the driver in the truck. This is a challenge, given how the man behaved. The strength of the heart can be judged by the amount of resistance you have to immediately opening to a place of compassion and forgiveness. How easy is it for you to say, or consider saying, the following? "I know that the driver's behavior comes from a place of his own pain. That man must have been suffering in some way, because it is our pain that makes us not respect the dignity of other. I can open my heart to him, have compassion for him, even though I have no idea what his pain is about. I can forgive him for his actions, and in doing so, I free myself from any of his negative energy."

Notice once again, that in forgiving, you are not condoning the man's irresponsible actions, and that you would still want to take steps to be sure that you were not hurt by them, or subjected to them, in any way.

The heart is the place where any negative emotions from the second energy center can be transformed into the higher vibrations of compassion. If we do not use the heart as a transformer, our statements will read like this: "I will never forgive that nasty so-and-so. He could have hurt me! Opening my heart would be stupid! It makes me vulnerable, and then what would happen with a nasty person around? That guy doesn't deserve my compassion. I am only compassionate and loving to people who are kind and loving toward me."

The next place the energy of the event travels is to the fifth energy center, at the throat. The fifth center contains the energy of the will and the ability to communicate and speak up for oneself. If it is healthy, it is interested in the truth about the event in the parking lot, even if that truth includes how your own negative beliefs attracted the experience. You use your will energy to make choices to support your positive forward movement, you determine your response (rather than engaging in reactionary behavior) and you direct energy to support the heart to be open.

If the fifth center is distorted, you will be critical and judgmental about the driver of the truck, and call him as many names as he called you. In cahoots with a distorted second energy center, your fifth center may demand the "justice" of seeing the driver punished, hurt or made powerless in some way for his negative behavior. Or you may struggle with your inability to speak up for yourself about the experience. Angry statements may come out of your throat center, as the untransformed energy of the event continues through your system.

It is the job of the sixth energy center, also called the third eye, to see the event on deeper levels than you ordinarily do. The sixth center is about insight and seeing events symbolically. Now you begin to move into the belief that this test was an opportunity for growth, and was provided by Spirit, even though it felt very uncomfortable and upsetting. You can only move in this direction if the fifth energy center *is willing to do so*. Energy from the will must be directed toward the higher vibrational levels of the sixth energy center to provoke insight and growth. The task of the sixth center is to see the situation so clearly, that you empower yourself with an understanding of your connection to

Spirit. In accomplishing this, you are able to comfort and uplift others so that they can similarly empower themselves.

The healthy sixth center also pulls you out of denial about your own defensive behavior. It opens your eyes to see how holding your energy aligned with negative beliefs will attract certain people into your life and promote a certain outcome. It allows you to see and define your own inappropriate patterns of behavior, thought and speech.

The distorted sixth energy center will ask: "Why does this keep happening to me? Why do I have to go through painful, uncomfortable situations? Life is not fair." When these statements are made, it is quite easy to move into the seventh energy center with the statement: "God does not care about me."

The belief that God does not care about you immediately leads you to the illusion that you are quite separate from God and that the universe is hostile. Life, then, becomes a burden, something to be endured or run away from. You feel powerless, unsafe, and unsupported. Nothing makes much sense and you lose any belief in the existence of a Castle of Light. All of life seems to be the Forest of Thorns.

If the seventh center is open, you have very different perceptions. You understand that there is a Divine Plan guiding you moment by moment. You feel a connection to Spirit that will see you through times of great test and trial. You have access to expanded states of awareness in which you continually come to terms with human existence; you carry the energy of faith and trust in a Greater Power. You open the doorway to allow grace to come into your life. You realize that life is a miracle.

If the experience has moved through your energy centers unhampered by negative beliefs, it is at the seventh center where you will let it go. You no longer need to worry about it, feel uncomfortable about it or hold onto it in any way. You are supported by Spirit. The hand of God is in your life.

Think back over the situation and identify the positive and negative perceptions you would hold if such an event occurred to you. This will help you to understand the places in which you need to do further exploration.

Now go back to the description of the event and once again place yourself in the scene and allow yourself to imagine your feelings and thoughts about what happened. Allow yourself the familiar feeling of being wronged, of feeling powerless, of being angry, of needing justice and not getting it. Hold those feelings and the thoughts they engender as something more is added to the story, something you did not know before.

What if you are now told that two weeks ago, the man driving the truck lost his only beloved child to a drug overdose, and that the man's heart was energetically broken in two? What if you were told that this man was so grief-stricken that he had driven into the grocery store parking lot and had to drive right out again, as he realized that the simple task of shopping was too much to ask of him right then? What if you now found out that this man felt completely powerless, was angry at God and at the world for the loss of his son and was overwhelmingly frightened that the reason his son died was that he had not been a good enough father to his child?

What is happening to your energy? Are you feeling your heart open? Have some different feelings begun to flow? Has the additional information allowed any negatively-charged emotions you were purposely holding to be transformed into compassion and forgiveness? Are you experiencing the alchemical ability of your heart and the power of love and compassion — not in condoning another's negative actions, but in understanding another's pain? If you stay with the feeling, you may experience your energy field flooding with the pure Light of our common Spirit.

Does getting this additional information let the driver of the truck off the hook for his negative and possibly dangerous actions and words? Not at all. It may *explain* the driver's behavior, but he is still one hundred percent accountable for his actions. Does it mean that you have to allow someone to disrespect you or make you uncomfortable or frightened? Again, the answer is no. The added part of the story simply allows you to understand that when we act out, it comes from a place of pain, fear, and forgetting that God is always with us, no matter how hard the trials we go through.

Here is the difficult question: Can we be compassionate *without* knowing the whole story? Can we keep our hearts open as a habit, rather than as an exception? We all need the experience of opening our hearts. We all need to *seek out those experiences* which allow the energies of love, compassion and forgiveness to flow through us. In so doing we metabolize the energies of the crucible of the heart. Are we ready to take the lesson of the Piscean Age into the new millennium? Are we ready to use our hearts to begin to heal our wounds, to begin to heal our lives, to begin to heal the planet?

GATHERING
THE GIFTS

◆

Karma's heartbeat.
Let it come full circle in me.
I shall spit out chain and bondage
and teach the freeing things
to come home.

I came for this very task:
to gather only the gifts.

BURIED TREASURE

I once worked with a young woman who had had a difficult childhood. She was having trouble feeling any connection with God in her
life. She *knew* God was there, but she could not *feel* the presence of
Spirit. The woman was a massage therapist and one day she was invit-
ed, as part of a group of massage therapists, to visit an orphanage and
give massages to some of the children. As she performed her work, she
felt strong emotions surging through her, something she was not used
to, and had not allowed in many years. Afterwards, she went into a
small enclosed garden and sat by herself for over an hour, alternately
weeping deeply and being very still. She later reported to me: "Nancy,
at the end of the hour I had the most extraordinary thought! I knew in
the core of my heart that grace can enter our lives through our
wounds."

That insight gives us an opening through which we are finally able
to encounter our dragons and begin to understand that any traumatic
experience encompasses not only the pain of a wound, but also the sav-
ing grace of Spirit. The grace, which lays buried beneath our pain, can
be upwelled to flood our wounds with transformational energy. When
this happens, the facts of any difficult history remain the same, but our

attitude toward our history — our perception and definition of it — changes.

In this way we are able to reconnect with Spirit very strongly. There is no linear explanation for what happens; we only know that we begin to feel the presence of Divine Light in our lives. This Light illuminates qualities we embody, some of which we have been completely unaware. We feel stronger, more whole, more at peace. Negative beliefs, which have been born from our wounds, dissolve and are replaced with beliefs of a higher vibration.

This kind of healing experience comes from a profound and seemingly paradoxical idea: that our wounds can bear treasure, that something which hurts can contain gold. This would mean that there are much deeper and different interpretations of events than we are used to assigning. Our job is to journey through the unexplored underworld in order to retrieve the bounty.

We seem to be back to the hero's journey, back to the quest of the initiatory experience that broadens and deepens our sight and brings healing to our life. We once again touch on the astounding possibility that it is through the vehicle of our tests, trials and trauma that we can recognize the miracle of who we really are. Looking through these eyes, we are given an opportunity to redefine crisis, disease and pain as chariots that can convey us to our destiny of freedom and magnificence.

Spinning Straw into Gold

In the previous section, we discussed how the tests we experience get us in shape so that we can fulfill our destiny, complete our divine task. It is an important attribute of our evolving self-awareness to accept our lives as being continually beneficent. A significant step in our growth is when we are able to know that a painful experience contains the blessings of Spirit in the form of precise direction and guidance from our guardian angel.

Fulfilling our destiny is the reason we are here in a body, on this planet. It is many people's fear that they will not fulfill their destiny before they die or, worse yet, they will never even know what it is.

Actually, we can get a lot of clues about our divine task by noticing the places in our life where things flow smoothly and where they do not. Our attributes and talents, our inherent qualities and the things that make our life easy, are gifts we have brought with us into the body to facilitate the fulfillment of our task. The places where we seem to be continually tested, constantly lacking, are areas where we need to learn something completely and consciously in order to fulfill our destiny. It is these seemingly deficient places that we need to explore because they are the sites of buried treasure, treasure which will astonish and delight us because it is not only ours to keep, but it more clearly and broadly defines who we are.

If we remember the Law of Polarity, we know that things that seem to be opposite are really two points on one circular continuum, and one can be transformed into the other. Trauma becomes treasure, lack becomes fulfillment, chaos becomes serenity. The qualities that seem the most unreachable for us, the most alien to us, are inevitably the ones we need to satisfy our soul's longing. What we are most afraid of, what we believe we can never have – these are exactly the places where we must focus. The idea of spinning gold from straw is exactly the attitude we are asked to develop no matter how absurd and impossible it seems. The very things we know nothing about will be the places where we become so strong that we give out our strength to the world.

FULFILLING OUR DESTINY

We come into the physical body birthed from Spirit and therefore carry the seeds of every single divine quality that exists, just as we carry genes from our physical parents. All we need to do in order to develop every quality is to nurture and cultivate the seeds. But it is the human experience that, in the density of the physical condition, we forget that we have these seeds to cultivate and we do not believe that we can develop the qualities that would make us magnificent, divinely powerful human beings.

Our soul's task will involve cultivating specific divine attributes. Other attributes will come easily to us. When the mandala of our soul's longing reflects that our task in this lifetime is to achieve mastery in a specific area, we will most likely be born into an environment where that mastery is not allowed, not known, or considered too threatening to even attempt. As we grow up, our family and other influential groups will not model for us how to develop this mastery, and any attempts we make will probably immediately be discouraged and squelched. This is not because our family, or other groups, are bad; it is because we need to learn something from scratch. We need to break through all barriers to know every nuance, every detail, every particular, every step, with regard to the conscious development of what it is we are to master.

We know the area where we are to achieve mastery from the very moment of our birth. We may not know it consciously, but it is configured in our energetic make-up. We carry the configuration in our upper chest, between the desire center (in the throat) and the heart center. At some level, even as children, we know *exactly what it is we need to achieve in order to fulfill the heart's desire that is our destiny*.

However, being children, we soon accept our family's beliefs and we may give up trying to upwell the divine characteristics we came into the body to develop. We may suppress our longing in an attempt to not feel the pain of its deficit. But because we carry the imprint of our task, it is always nudging us. On some level, it speaks to us, and we feel it, although we are probably not able to describe or define it, and it may simply feel like an irritating emptiness. We dream about our longing even when it is nameless, and we begin to try to fill our empty ache with material goods, relationships, careers, and other diversions, none of which are able to quench our thirst for our true desire.

The Negative Statements for Abandoning Our Quest

The absence of the divine qualities we need to cultivate is accepted by us on a superficial level, and we have many reasons why we should not and cannot even consider developing these qualities. These reasons surface when we see the qualities in someone else, or when the itch of our longing threatens to break through into our conscious minds and begin rearranging our life.

The negative statements for not cultivating the divine qualities we feel we lack come from distortions in each of the seven centers of our energetic body. From the root, or first energy center, we say: "Having this quality is simply not allowed, not accepted, not supported, not safe." This underlines the belief systems of our family and/or society. From the second center comes the statement: "I am not powerful enough to develop this quality," and from the third energy center we say: "I do not deserve to have this quality in my life."

The fourth center of the heart convinces us that we do not really love and adore the idea of upwelling the divine qualities we lack and achieving the mastery we crave. It would be too troublesome, too difficult. It would change our life too much when it does not need to change at all. This longing of our heart is silly and frivolous and the best thing to do is just not to feel it. The fifth energy center of the will and desire simply says: "I will not even try; I will not allow myself to desire it." The sixth center of linear thinking convinces us that there is no sound reason to develop these qualities. The voice of our intuition from the sixth center is silenced or ignored. The seventh center, from which we secretly pray to be able to master the divine characteristics we long for, tells us that our prayers are not heard and God is not that interested anyway.

But even with all this confusion, illusion and negativity cast around the idea of heading in the direction in which our longing is propelling us, the truth of the matter is that we came into the body specifically for this task. In our heart of hearts, all we really want to do on this planet is to become proficient and graceful in the mastery we long for.

Transformation and Resolution

How does a situation like this ever resolve itself? Our subconscious mind, ever amenable to suggestion from our waking mind and all the statements, thoughts and resistances it has about following our longing, obeys the directives from the distorted statements and makes sure that in our life, we have not even a whisper of what our heart desires. This becomes a tremendously painful situation and compromises the flow patterns of our energy body, which was actually set up to perfectly accommodate the flourishing growth and mastery of the divine qualities we need to develop.

The resolution can come in several ways. We may be aware enough to recognize that something feels misaligned in our lives and freely agree to explore what it is. This is akin to volunteering for the hero's journey even though it scares us to death. Death in this case will be our rebirth into a transformed and healthier person. We will be asked to move through all the negative configurations and face our monsters in order to transform them into what they were originally meant to be — a stairway that takes us to the top of the mountain.

However, many times, in order to embark upon an initiatory path of conscious evolution, we need a bit more urging. This is where discomfort, crisis and disease come in. Because we want them to go away, these unpleasant conditions are strong incentives to go into the heart of what we have been avoiding for so long, and realize that the only way *out* is *through*.

In examining, witnessing, feeling, embracing and loving the parts of us that have continually told us why we should not and could not develop the divine attributes we crave, we open an energetic passageway in the body for our longing to emerge. This emergence is part of our healing and provides an underlying support for the transformed patterns in the energy field. The emerging longing holds the energy field in perfect balance and alignment with the task we came into the body to carry out.

At some point in the transformation process, we are awed by the perfection and precision with which Spirit teaches us what we need to learn. Whatever our crisis, we come to terms with it and begin to sense that it was personalized for us so that we could finally become whole.

And when we look back over our shoulder at our life, we begin to sense that *every single moment in our life* has been leading us to the insights that we have recovered. We realize that *every single moment Spirit has been directing us, teaching us, preparing us and loving us.* When we finally find the pathway which leads us to our destiny, we find that not only do we have all the tools to fulfill our task, but also that we are *perfectly suited* to carry it out.

In our healing process, the process of becoming all that we really are, we take full responsibility for all the choices we have made, as well as the subsequent consequences of those choices, including pain felt by others because of our actions. Owning that responsibility takes courage. We must make the commitment to have all action from that moment on be aligned with Divine Law. We must strive to balance past negative actions with positive thoughts, words and deeds. This is how we begin to work with our karmic debt. As we do this, we again begin to realize that *there was not one arbitrary moment in our lives*, whatever the paths we have taken. The choices we made were transformational opportunities, and our judgment of those choices now as "positive" or "negative" is irrelevant. Blame, of ourselves and others, is not applicable. The only thing that is beneficial to assess is our present state of consciousness. Whether the road we have taken was straight and short, or bumpy and circuitous, our job is to understand how it provided us with exactly what we needed in order to evolve into the waiting hands of our divine objective.

The Transformational Statements

The fact that we can believe for so long that fulfilling our longing is not available for us makes the act of finally doing it that much sweeter. We will know the process of achieving it intimately. We will view that process as sacred. We will cultivate and bloom our divine characteristics over and over again for the sheer pleasure of it and by our very actions, we will help others, who also need to cultivate these characteristics, learn how to take the risks to do so.

If our longing does not yet have words, we can make it a focus of our meditation to upwell the sensation of it in our body. Then we affirm the following statements, which are the transformation of the distorted statements from the energy centers.

1. My life/my longing is accepted and supported.

2. I have all the power I will ever need, right now, to carry out my longing.

3. I am worthy of the gift my longing will bring.

4. I can express my longing through my love; I can express my love through my longing.

5. I am willing to create my longing.

6. My longing is the reason I incarnated.

7. My longing is part of the universe's Divine Plan.

If we dare to look more deeply into the painful aspects of our experiences, we find the inherent gift in each. Our crisis is merely the Forest of Thorns which will lead us to the Castle of Light. All the while that we feel we are lost and defenseless, we need only to ask to receive the impenetrable shield, the magic sword, the valiant steed and the wise guidance of our spirit helpers. If we can believe in the gift, our challenging journey through the Forest becomes not only meaningful, but heroic.

Writer and artist Patricia Spear wrote: "[Our crisis] may be physically excruciating, mentally incomprehensible and emotionally devastating. But spiritually, in some way, it is perfect." If we can allow it, if we can surrender to the fact that we do not see as broadly as Spirit sees, do not know as Spirit knows, we will be carried by Spirit into the perfection.

THE HEROIC JOURNEYS
OF CHILDREN

We all know of stories of devastating childhoods, stories that can make us weep with the weight of the words that fall upon our ears and pierce our hearts. We know of those who came through such childhoods and have worked to become strong and whole. And we see the road littered with those who were devoured and crushed.

Childhood tragedy seems especially painful because children are so vulnerable, so at the mercy of their environments. The trauma some experience as children is so incomprehensible that we will never be able to make linear sense of it. This is true for any tragedy; there is no way to "explain it away," nor should we even try. Our language does not presently contain vocabulary that can convey to us the coming-to-terms with tragedy which an expanded consciousness and the intervention of Divine grace can bring.

The tragedy that occurs in childhood can wound us deeply and it can be a long climb out of the pit. It is sometimes difficult to accept that the hand of God was behind the tests and trials of innocents. It is an act of utmost faith to believe that in sifting through the broken bones and broken psyches that the cruelty and ignorance we may have encountered during childhood can produce, we can find a treasure. It is hard to believe that broken flesh and silent screams can be transformed into hymns of life, and indeed, are meant to be. It seems impossible to believe that it is ever necessary to learn our lessons so harshly.

We must transcend the personality in order to come to terms with what happens on this planet. We must pray for strong hearts, strong wills and divine understanding that will move us forward into a place of acceptance and forgiving when events make no sense and seem profoundly severe. We must trust that, no matter what happens, we are never abandoned by Spirit, and that, especially as children, we are lifted into Spirit's arms during times of tragedy, and there we are loved and protected.

Every child who undergoes trauma, who is deprived of a nurturing physical and emotional upbringing, is provided with a spiritual upbringing that produces a connection with Spirit that is both resilient and powerful. The child's consciousness is lifted from the physical body and the physical plane and brought to a place of Light where the child is soothed and taught by emissaries of Spirit who bestow a wisdom and understanding beyond the child's earth-life years. This connection is not always remembered as the child becomes an adult. But if it can be brought back in some way, it many times provides the lifeline that the adult needs to climb out of a nightmare.

Trauma is an opening to an initiatory journey. Those who choose to go through such journeys as children are courageous souls who want the opportunity to move swiftly and deeply into the quest for consciousness and union with a Divine Source while on the earth. We must remember that the age of the soul does not match the age of the physical body. The soul of a child can be eons old, and at all times the soul is being guided and provided for.

The phrase, the "wounded healer," refers to the person who has moved through his or her wounds into wholeness, and nowhere is this more apparent than in adults who have healed tragic childhoods. The word "healer" does not refer to an occupation, but rather to energetic configurations that the adult carries. These configurations send the message that no matter how black, how deep, how tragic our pasts, we can emerge victorious. The message tells us that, as deeply as any of us have ever known pain, just as deeply can we now know grace.

NOTICING WHAT IS GOOD

We need not have had terrible trauma in our life to embark upon the hero's journey. The journey is offered any time we are willing to make the leap into a more expanded consciousness. We want to keep ourselves always ready to embark, and one way to do this is to develop the habit of noticing the good things in life. In this way, we strengthen ourselves in preparation for our hero's journey, whenever the opportunity should arise.

In the section on the creative process, we noticed that it is a human characteristic to focus on what is wrong with our lives, rather than on what is right, to focus on our pain rather than our peace. If the Aquarian Magician focuses on pain and negativity, then that is what he will grow in his garden. If, however, he draws down the peace and happiness that are possible in life, his garden bears different fruit. To cultivate a habit of noticing what is good in life, and to give thanks for it, can be a powerful transformational tool. What we notice need not be flashy; in fact, it will probably be profoundly simple. The act of bringing to mind and appreciating the simple gifts — the warmth of the sun on our face, the sound of gentle rain, remembering an instance of grace in our life — will reap blessing and a kind of fortune that can never be lost.

To find treasure, we must know the many guises that treasure can take. Otherwise, we can walk right by our bounty without recognizing it. If we practice noticing small treasures on a daily basis, we can become experts in recovering wealth. Once again, we must go far beyond what is normally defined as valuable by expanding our definition and broadening our sight to include all the blessings and favors that are around us and inside of us simply because we are children of a Divine Force.

STEPPING INTO AQUARIUS

You have come to this planet, born of magnificent Divine parents, for a specific reason. That reason is cloaked in Divine energy. You have come to fulfill a destiny which is crucial to your soul's growth. You are here on this planet at this moment because you have chosen to be here at a time when the physical plane provides one of the best opportunities for high-speed growth of consciousness. Whatever your past, your future depends upon the intention you set and the choices you make *in this very moment*. All your power is right here, right now.

Your hero's journey is inevitable. If you are in human form, you have a journey in your future, whether that be in one second, or ten years. Your hero's journey is like a ship that is waiting for you when you are ready to sail. It is a ship that is guided by Spirit, by the Will-to-Good that creates the universe. It is a ship that will take you on a journey that will change your life. The journey will open your eyes to reveal to you the truth of who you really are. On your journey, you will have to learn about the power of love and compassion, or your ship will be lost at sea. Welcome your journey with open arms, even if the prospect of it frightens you. We all are frightened some times.

Prepare yourself for the journey. Learn to recognize Spirit everywhere around you. Learn to see Spirit in the people you dislike. Remember that we are all connected so that what you contribute to the energy web is positive and uplifting. Be grateful for what is good in life; begin to notice it more and more. Contribute to what is good by acts of kindness and love. These habits will strengthen you so that, once you embark, you do not falter.

Remember that Spirit is the Will-to-Good. Trust that there exists a Divine Love for you that is so strong, one tiny taste of It can change your life. Believe in the Force of Love.

Let it carry you Home.

NOTES

SPIRIT AND SCIENCE: THE ONE
FORCE AND THE WEB OF LIFE

1. Manly Hall, *Secret Teachings of All Ages* (Los Angeles: Philosophical Research Society, Inc., 1977), p. XXI.

2. Dr. Ann Davies, *Builders of the Adytum Audiocassette Astrology Series* (Los Angeles: Builders of the Adytum, Los Angeles, 1985). Builders of the Adytum, 5101-05 North Figueroa Street, Los Angeles, CA, is an international, non-profit, teaching and training Order and an outer vehicle of the Inner School, which guides the evolution of humanity. (323) 255-7141. Website: http://bota.org.

3. Sir Isaac Newton, the renown late-seventeenth-century scientist upon whose findings Newtonian physics is based, was himself a very spiritual man. He was interested in alchemy, and called the Life Spirit "ether." He believed this ether existed in the human body, giving it life and movement; however, because there was no scientific proof of its existence, Newton did not attempt to include it in his description of the Universe.

4. There is controversy over whether these words were actually spoken by Chief Seattle. His speech was said to be transcribed by an early Seattle settler, Dr. Henry Smith, who took notes as the great chief spoke in the Suquamish dialect. There are sources which state that the sentences quoted here were actually added to the original speech by Ted Perry in

1970, for an environmental movie called *Home*. Whatever the case, the statements accurately reflect the spiritual and environmental philosophy of the native Americans.

5. Werner Heisenberg, *Physics and Philosophy* (New York: Harper Torchbooks, 1958), p. 107.
6. Daniel C. Matt, *The Essential Kabbalah: The Heart of Jewish Mysticism* (New York: HarperCollins Publishers, 1996), p. 26.
7. From *The Tao of Physics* by Fritjof Capra © 1975, 1983, 1991, 1999. Reprinted by arrangement with Shambhala Publications, Inc., Boston MA. www.shambhala.com.
8. Capra, p. 188.
9. David Bohm, *Parts of a Whole*, New Dimensions Foundation audiocassette interview with Michael Toms (Boulder, CO: Sounds True, 1988).
10. Black Elk was an Oglala Sioux holy man who lived from 1863 to 1950. His story is told in John G. Neihardt's *Black Elk Speaks: Being the Life Story of a Holy Man of the Oglala Sioux* (Lincoln, NB: University of Nebraska Press, 1979).

THE PHYSICS OF ANCIENT WISDOM: UNIVERSAL LAW

11. Six of the seven laws we explore are set forth by Three Initiates, *The Kybalion, A Study of the Hermetic Philosophy of Ancient Egypt and Greece*, (Chicago: The Yogi Publication Society, 1940).
12. C.G. Jung, *Memories, Dreams and Reflections* (New York: Vintage Books, 1989), p. 335.
13. Fred Hoyle, *Frontiers of Astronomy* (New York: HarperCollins Publishers, 1955), p. 304.
14. Three Initiates, p. 171.

ENERGY LITERACY

15. David Bohm, *Wholeness and the Implicate Order* (New York: Routledge, 1980), p. 2.
16. Thorwald Dethlefsen and Rudiger Dahlke, *The Healing Power of Illness: The Meaning of Symptoms and How to Interpret Them* (Rockport, MA: Element Books, 1991), p. 9.
17. For specific information on energy field research see Dr. Richard Gerber's book, *Vibrational Medicine* (Santa Fe, NM: Bear & Company, 1988).
18. For more specific information on human energy field interaction, see Barbara Ann Brennan's *Light Emerging* (New York: Bantam Books, 1993).
19. Both sounds and colors have specific frequencies and can raise or

lower the vibratory rate in a person's energy field.

20. Davies, *B.O.T.A. Audiocassette Astrology Series.*

THE SYNERGISTIC COMMUNITY OF
THE HUMAN ENERGY FIELD

21. See Brennan, *Hands of Light* (New York: Bantam Books, 1987), Chapter 7, for specific locations of the energy centers.
22. I learned the pelvic rotation exercise at the Barbara Brennan School of Healing in the late 1980s.
23. Dethlefsen and Dahlke, Chapter Four, Part Two.
24. Brennan, Chapter 9.
25. Brennan, Chapter 9.

SYMBOLIC INTERPRETATION: FINDING
SPIRITUAL DIRECTIVES IN EVERYDAY LIFE

26. Natalie Goldberg, *Writing Down the Bones* (Boston: Shambhala Publications, Inc., 1986), p. 8-10.
27. Caroline Casey, *Making the Gods Work for You* (New York: Harmony Books, 1998).
28. This is a variation of a Eugene T. Gendlin's focusing technique presented in his book, *Focusing* (New York: Bantam Books, 1981).
29. This question, and the two derivative questions that follow, are based on questions from Dethlefsen and Dahlke, p. 82.
30. This metaphor for meditating is set forth in a Builders of the Adytum lesson on Tarot Key Seventeen. Builders of the Adytum, 5101 North Figueroa Street, Los Angeles, CA 90042, (323) 255-7141. Website: http://bota.org.

THE CREATIVE PROCESS

31. Reprinted with permission from Builders of the Adytum, 5105 North Figueroa Street, Los Angeles, California 90042, (323) 255-7141. Website: http://bota.org.

THE HEART OF THE MATTER

32. Caroline Myss, *Anatomy of the Spirit: The Seven Stages of Power and Healing* (New York: Harmony Books, 1996).
33. *Spirituality & Health*, Winter 1999, p. 33.

SELECTED BIBLIOGRAPHY

Arroyo, Stephen. *Astrology, Psychology and the Four Elements: An Energy Approach to Astrology and Its Use in the Counseling Arts.* Reno, NV: CRCS Publications, 1975.

Bailey, Alice A. *Esoteric Astrology.* New York: Lucis Publishing, 1951.

—————. *Esoteric Healing.* New York: Lucis Publishing, 1953.

Bohm, David. *Parts of a Whole.* Audio tape recording. New Dimensions Foundation interview with Michael Toms. Boulder, CO: Sounds True, 1988.

—————. *Wholeness and the Implicate Order.* New York: Routledge, 1980.

Burt, Kathleen. *Archetypes of the Zodiac.* St. Paul, MN: Llewellyn Publications, 1996.

Brennan, Barbara Ann. *Hands of Light: A Guide to Healing Through the Human Energy Field.* New York: Bantam Books, 1987.

—————. *Light Emerging: The Journal of Personal Healing.* New York: Bantam Books, 1993.

Bruyere, Rosalyn L. *Wheels of Light: A Study of the Chakras.* Arcadia, CA: Bon Productions, 1989.

Campbell, Joseph. *The Inner Reaches of Outer Space.* New York: Harper & Row, 1986.

————. *The Power of Myth*. New York: Doubleday, 1988.

Capra, Fritjof. *The Tao of Physics*. New York: Bantam Books, 1984.

Case, Paul Foster. *Highlights of Tarot*. Los Angeles: Builders of the Adytum, 1984.

Casey, Caroline W. *Inner and Outer Space: The Astrological Language of the Psyche*. Audio tape recording. Boulder, CO: Sounds True, 1996.

————. *Making the Gods Work for You: The Astrological Language of the Psyche*. New York: Harmony Books, 1998.

Cooper, David A. *The Mystical Kabbalah*. Audio tape recording. Boulder, CO: Sounds True, 1994.

Dethlefsen, Thorwald and Rudiger Dahlke. *The Healing Power of Illness: The Meaning of Symptoms and How to Interpret Them*. Rockport, MA: Element Books Limited, 1991.

Eliade, Mircea. *A History of Religious ideas, Volume 1*. Chicago: University of Chicago Press, 1978.

Encyclopaedia Britannica CD 98 Multimedia Edition. CD-ROM. Encyclopaedia Britannica, Inc. 1994-1998.

Gendlin, Eugene T. *Focusing*. New York: Bantam Books, 1981.

Gerber, Richard. *Vibrational Medicine: New Choices for Healing Ourselves*. Santa Fe, NM: Bear & Company, 1988.

Goldberg, Natalie. *Writing Down the Bones: Freeing the Writer Within*. Boston: Shambhala Publications, 1986.

Halevi, Z'ev ben Shimon. *Kabbalah: The Divine Plan*. York Beach, ME: Samuel Weiser, Inc., 1974.

————. *Introduction to the Cabala*. York Beach, ME: Samuel Weiser, Inc., 1972.

Hall, Manly P. *The Secret Teachings of All Ages*. Los Angeles: The Philosophical Research Society, Inc., 1978.

Heisenberg, Werner. *Physics and Philosophy*. New York: Harper Torchbooks, 1958.

Hickey, Isabel M. *Astrology: A Cosmic Science*. Sebastopol, CA: CRCS Publications, 1992.

Hitching, Francis. *Earth Magic.* New York: William Morrow and Company, 1977.

Howell, Alice O. *Jungian Symbolism in Astrology.* Wheaton, IL: The Theosophical Publishing House, 1987.

————. *Jungian Synchronicity in Astrological Signs and Ages.* Wheaton: IL: Quest Books, 1990.

Jansky, Robert Carl. *Astrology, Nutrition and Health.* Atglen, PA: Whitford Press, 1977.

Jung, C.G. *Memories, Dreams, Reflections.* New York: Vintage Books, 1989.

Kurtz, Ron and Hector Prestera. *The Body Reveals: What Your Body Says About You.* New York: Harper & Row, 1976.

Matt, Daniel C. *The Essential Kabbalah: The Heart of Jewish Mysticism.* San Francisco: HarperCollins, 1996.

Meece, E. Alan. *Horoscope for the New Millennium.* St. Paul, MN: Llewellyn Publications, 1997.

Mishlove, Jeffrey. *The Roots of Consciousness: Psychic Liberation through History, Science and Experience.* New York: Random House, 1975.

Myss, Caroline. *Anatomy of the Spirit: The Seven Stages of Power and Healing.* New York: Harmony Books, 1996.

————. *Why People Don't Heal and How They Can.* New York: Harmony Books, 1997.

Narby, Jeremy. *The Cosmic Serpent: DNA and the Origins of Knowledge.* New York: Jeremy P. Tarcher, 1998.

Neihardt, John G. *Black Elk Speaks: Being the Life Story of a Holy Man of the Oglala Sioux.* Lincoln, NE: University of Nebraska Press, 1979.

Neumann, Erich. *The Origins and History of Consciousness.* Princeton, NJ: Princeton University Press, 1954.

Nhat Hanh, Thich. *Touching Peace: Practicing the Art of Mindful Living.* Berkeley, CA: Parallax Press, 1992.

Nichols, Sallie. *Jung and Tarot: An Archetypal Journey.* York Beach, ME: Samuel Weiser, Inc., 1980.

Oken, Alan. *Alan Oken's Complete Astrology.* New York: Bantam Books, 1980.

————. *Soul-Centered Astrology: A Key to Your Expanding Self*. Freedom, CA: The Crossing Press, 1996.

Olesky, Rio. *Astrology and Consciousness: The Wheel of Light*. Tempe, AZ: New Falcon Publications, 1995.

Parry, Danaan. *Warriors of the Heart: A Handbook for Conflict Resolution*. Cooperstown, NY: Sunstone Publications, 1991.

Rudhyar, Dane. *An Astrological Triptych: The Illumined Road*. Santa Fe, NM: Aurora Press, 1968.

————. *The Astrological Houses: The Spectrum of Individual Experience*. Sebastopol, CA: CRCS Publications, 1972.

Russell, Peter. *The Global Brain Awakens: Our Next Evolutionary Leap*. Palo Alto, CA: Global Brain, Inc., 1995.

Shealy, C. Norman, and Caroline M. Myss. *The Creation of Health*. Walpole, NH: Stillpoint Publishing, 1993.

Sheldrake, Rupert. *A New Science of Life*. Los Angeles: J.P. Tarcher, 1981.

————. *A New Science of Life*. Audio tape recording. New Dimensions Foundation interview with Michael Toms. Boulder, CO: Sounds True, 1990.

Simpkinson, Charles and Anne Simpkinson, eds. *Sacred Stories: A Celebration of the Power of Stories to Transform and Heal*. San Francisco: HarperSanFrancisco, 1993.

Three Initiates. *The Kybalion: Hermetic Philosophy*. Chicago: The Yogi Publication Society, 1940.

Tresidder, Jack. *Dictionary of Symbols: An Illustrated Guide to Traditional Images, Icons, and Emblems*. San Francisco: Chronicle Books, 1998.

Wright, Machaelle Small. *Behaving As If the God in All Life Mattered: A New Age Ecology*. Jeffersonton, VA: Perelandra, 1987.

INDEX

A

Age of Aquarius, 233–4
  Age of Energy, 76–77
  ancient wisdom, 10–17, 24–36,
  creative process, 171–95
  destiny, fulfilling, 223–28
  energy literacy, 75–101
  global community, 42
  glyph, 32, 50
  heart, power of, 197–218
  human energy field, 103–48
  Inventor archetype, 15
  Magician archetype, 231
  science, 14–23, 32–36
  symbolic interpretation,
    149–69
  transforming wounds, 220–22
  Universal Law, 37–74
  Uranus, modern ruling planet, 13,
    20
Age of Aries, 11, 74
  Mars, mythological god, 120
  Mars, ruling planet, 120
  Warrior, 120
Age of Cancer, 11, 25, 40

  Great Mother, 11
Age of Gemini, 54
  Mercury, mythological god, 54
Age of Pisces, 10, 12, 198
  Mystic, 10, 13, 42
  science, 18
Age of Taurus, 11
ancient wisdom, 10-17, 24-36, 38,
  42, 48, 59, 61, 76, 77
  relationship with modern physics,
    14–17
Anderson, Carl, 54
anorexia, 58
archetypes, 161
  Great Mother, 11
  Inventor, 15
  Magician, 231
  Mystic, 10, 13, 42
  Warrior, 120
as above, so below, 20, 43
astrological ages, 1
astrology, 1
astrophysics, 20
auric field. *See* human energy field

B

belief systems, 89, 105–8, 141-43,
    178, 192, 212
Black Elk, 29
Bohm, David, 21-22, 27
Bohr, Niels, 44
Brennan, Barbara, 27, 139, 190-91
Bruyere, Rosalyn, 152
bulimia, 58

C

Campbell, Joseph, 118
Cana wedding feast, 49
Capra, Fritjof, 19, 34
Casey, Caroline, 144, 158
Cooper, David, 152
cosmology, 20
creative process, 66, 171–95
    questions, 194-95
    subconsciousness, 181–83
    superconsciousness, 176–77
    waking consciousness, 178–79

D

Dahlke, Rudiger, 82
Dalai Lama, 210
defense mechanisms, 107
destiny, fulfilling, 223–228
Dethlefsen, Thorwald, 82
digestive system, 125-28
Dirac, Paul, 54
disease, 111
dissolution, 50–51
Divine Will, 136, 162
dogma, 13, 28
dynamism of life, 19–20, 31, 35,
    48, 78

E

Einstein, Albert, 15, 18

energy
    as a pervasive, living Force, 79–80
    as Spirit, 78–79
    directing, 92–95
    events as spiritual directives, 80–83
    interpenetration of fields, 86–87
    magnetic attraction, 88–89
    net, 84–85
    organization in fields, 85–86
    reading, 99–101
    representing the truth, 89–91
    vibrational rate, 97–99
energy centers, 44, 108-110,
    112–48, 224-25
    areas of the body, 112
    fifth, 115-116, 122, 136–40, 147,
        215, 225
    first, 110, 113–18, 121, 133, 138,
        142, 212, 224
    fourth, 120–21, 128, 130, 131–35,
        137, 139, 148, 199, 200–06,
        214–15, 224-25
    second, 119–23, 127, 133, 138–39,
        142, 212–13, 215, 224
    seventh, 117–18, 130, 146–48,
        177, 216, 225
    sixth, 100, 115, 141–45, 147,
        148, 185, 215–216, 225
    third, 115, 123, 124–30, 133–34,
        139, 142, 213-14, 224
evolution of consciousness, 1

F

feminine energy, 67–69
    distorted, 71–74

G

Gaia, 116
Gerber, Richard, 21
global community, 42
Goldman, Natalie, 157

H
healing crisis, 51
heart, power of, 197–218
Heisenberg, Werner, 16, 19
hero's journey, 221, 231, 233
    children's, 229–30
Higher Self, 129-30, 147, 148,
    176-77, 206
holistic model of human, 25
holography, 21
Hoyle, Fred, 46
human energy field, 44, 49, 50,
    85–87, 89–90, 103–48
    as community, 109–10
    as vehicle for Divinity, 105–06
    energy centers, 113–48
        fifth, 136–40
        first, 113–18
        fourth, 131–35
        second, 119–23
        seventh, 146–48
        sixth, 141–45
        third, 124–30
    holding life story, 104–05
    negative beliefs, 106–08
    structure, 108–09

I
implicate order, 21-22, 28-29
individuation, 116
initiation, 1
interconnectedness, 15, 20, 29–31,
    34–35, 41–42, 78, 84, 201
interface, 207
Internet, 35, 84
intuition, 144

J
Jesus of Nazareth, 49, 82
Jung, Carl, 45–46

Jupiter, 124–25, 127, 128, 134, 139

K
karma, 64–66, 90, 94
    tribal, 90
Kronos, 116
Kybalion, 53, 61, 62, 69

L
Law of Cause and Effect, 61–66, 202
    Law of Karma, 66–68, 94
Law of Correspondence, 43–47, 166
Law of Gender, 67–74, 92, 137
Law of One, 25, 36, 40–42, 47, 78,
    118, 212
Law of Polarity, 53–56, 57, 68, 222
Law of Rhythm, 57–60, 202
Law of Vibration, 19–20, 31, 48–52,
    55, 81
laying-on-of-hands, 50, 78
life task, 1, 90

M
Mars, 74, 120–22, 133, 137
masculine energy, 67–69
    undeveloped, 69–71
mass consciousness, 144
Matt, Daniel C., 16
meditation, 163–65
Mercury, 54, 146–47, 154
Middle Ages, 13, 24
modern physics, 14–23, 32–36, 48,
    77, 79, 80
    relationship with ancient wisdom,
        14–17
moon, 144
morphogenic field theory, 22
Myss, Caroline, 44-45, 204
mystery schools, 10–13, 14

N

Neolithic Revolution, 11
Newtonian physics, 15, 18, 19, 61, 76
nuclear force, 67

O

One Force, 12, 14, 28, 29, 40, 50, 70, 133, 135

P

Pert, Candace, 96
physics. *See* modern physics *and* Newtonian physics
Piscean-Aquarian interface, 207
Planck, Max, 19
planets, seven sacred, 110
polar opposites, 55
prayer, 94
psychoneuroimmunology, 21, 96, 110

Q

quantum theory, 18, 19–20

R

Reformation, 13
relativity theory, 18–20
rods and cones, 79
Roosevelt, Franklin D., 45

S

Saturn, 116, 133
Seattle, Chief, 16, 29, 35, 84
Sheldrake, Rupert, 22
Spear, Patricia, 228
subconsciousness, 115, 143, 157, 163, 175, 181–183, 184, 188
sun, 133
superconsciousness, 147, 176–77, 185

symbolic interpretation, 149–69
    irrational/illogical level, 162–67
    literal level, 154–55
    meaning/mystery level, 168–69
    outline, 150
    symbolic/metaphorical level, 156–61

T

Tarot
    Hermit Key, 148
    Key Fourteen, 209
    Magician Key, 147, 179, 180, 185–86

U

unity of life, 14, 18, 27–29, 35, 40–42
Universal Law, 37–74, 76, 160
    dissonance with, 39
    Law of Cause and Effect, 61–66, 202
    Law of Correspondence, 43–47, 166
    Law of Gender, 67–74, 137
    Law of One, 25, 40–42, 212
    Law of Polarity, 53–56, 222
    Law of Rhythm, 57–60, 202
    Law of Vibration, 19–20, 48–52
Uranus, 13, 20, 116

V

Venus, 74, 122, 137, 138

W

waking consciousness, 143, 147, 175, 178–79, 183, 184
Will-to-Good, 26, 27, 83, 169, 177, 208, 233, 234
writing practice, 157–58

NANCY PRIVETT is a writer, teacher and energy field therapist with over twenty-five years experience in the metaphysical arts and alternative healing. She studied with healer and author Barbara Brennan and is a graduate of the Brennan School of Healing. Ms. Privett is the founder and director of The Center for New Consciousness, located in eastern Long Island, New York, through which she has a private practice and teaches classes in the emerging consciousness of the new age.

Stepping Into the Aquarian Age
Ordering Information

Please send me _____ copies of *Stepping into the Aquarian Age: A Guidebook for the New Evolutionary Cycle* at $18.95 each plus $3.50 shipping for the first book and $1.00 for each additional book. New York residents add 8.25% sales tax.

Name:_____

Address: _____

City:_____State: _____ Zip: _____

Telephone: _____

E-Mail Address: _____

☐ Check or Money Order

Please charge my   ☐ Visa ☐ Master Card ☐ AMEX ☐ Discover

Card Number: _____   Exp. Date: ___ / ___

Signature:_____

Phone or Fax your order: (631) 325-3911

Please make your check payable and return to:
Old Lion Publishing
4 Montauk Highway
Westhampton, New York 11977

For information about upcoming workshops
please call (631) 325-3911